TRAV-EL-ATIONS

IT'S ABOUT PEOPLE,
NOT PLACES

Trav-el-ations

It's about people, not places

Konrad Brinck

TAMARIND TREE
Toronto

Copyright © 2019 Konrad Brinck

All rights reserved. No part of this publication may be reproduced, stored in a retrieval system or transmitted in any form or by any means, electronic, mechanical, photocopying, recording or otherwise, without the prior written permission of the publisher or the author. Inquiries should be addressed to:

    Tamarind Tree Books Inc.,
    14 Ferncastle Crescent,
    Brampton, Ontario. L7A 3P2, Canada.
        or
    Konrad Brinck,
    30 Parkside Drive,
    Brampton, Ontario, L6Y 2G9, Canada.

Brinck, Konrad, 1946-, author
Trav-el-lations : it's about people, not places / Konrad Brinck.

ISBN 978-1-989242-00-1 (pbk.)

1. Brinck, Konrad, 1946- --Travel. 2. Voyages around the world.
3. Voyages and travels--Anecdotes. I. Title. II. Title: Travellations.

G465.B74 2018   910.4'1092   C2018-906730 6

I am dedicating this book to all the travellers that have joined us on our many journeys, especially those who travelled with us to places far and wide and did not get their stories told in this book.

Special thanks to:
Horst and Maria Kliche for joining us on our Alaska cruise;
Gerry and Mybrit DeLeskie for joining us on our Baltic cruise;
Linda and Colin Hellens for travelling with us many times; and
John and Pat van Atter for being good company on many Canon trips.

Contents

FOREWORD		VIV
A FEW MORE WORDS...		X
INTRODUCTION		XI
Chapter 1 :	Travelling With Grandchildren	13
Chapter 2 :	Nightmare Of A Trip Gone Bad	21
Chapter 3 :	Bait And Switch In Bali	42
Chapter 4 :	Getting Shot In Mexico	45
Chapter 5 :	Laughing In Church?	49
Chapter 6 :	Fast Food In Peru	52
Chapter 7 :	Riding The Rails In Africa	55
Chapter 8 :	In Mexico 5x6 equals 40	61
Chapter 9 :	Samba In The Streets Of Rio	64
Chapter 10 :	Adventures Of A *Schlachtenbummler*	66
Chapter 11 :	What Americans Believe...	78
Chapter 12 :	Smoking And Drinking In Berlin	80
Chapter 13 :	Smoking And Drinking In Cairo	82
Chapter 14 :	My Travels With Tony	86
Chapter 15 :	My Day In A Mexican Jail	98
Chapter 16 :	The Final Journey	102

Foreword

Konrad Brinck is one of the smoothest storytellers I know.

Through his eyes we travel to unique destinations and taste, hear and smell the nitty-gritty of his adventures.

Be it samba in Rio, a rambunctious train-ride through the post-apartheid beauty of South Africa, the antics of World Soccer Cup fans in Germany, savouring the beauty and gastronomical delights of Europe, being touched to the heart by street children in Bali or exploring the pyramids and pharaohs of Egypt, Konrad keeps his readers entranced. His style is lyrical, personal and easy to enjoy. Whether he is telling amusing anecdotes about lovable street vendors eking out a living on tropical sidewalks or is describing agonizing pain from life's mishaps, as a reader I am totally hooked and cannot put the book down.

Along the way, his encounters provide good counsel for anyone who neglects to read insurance companies' small print. Travelling with his grandchildren is a glorious experience that tickles the heart of any reader who knows the joy of children and grandchildren and can appreciate the humor in the German words 'Ausfahrt' and 'Einfahrt'.

But Konrad also handles some very serious life-and-death issues using plain and honest language to poignantly tell what for many would be difficult to recount. Again, his style opens the reader's heart to see and appreciate the many layers of life.

This collection will take you on a revealing journey with smiles and laughter and some tears but with an accompanying touch of serenity.

Dr. Vicki Bismilla,
Author and retired Superintendent of Schools and College Vice-President Academic, Toronto.

A Few More Words...

Everyone experiences challenges in life, but few can tell their story like Konrad. Having already thoroughly enjoyed his first book, IT'S JUST ME! Brinck has taken his story-telling to a higher, even more enjoyable level.

His writing style, intrigue and humour draws you in and makes you want to read on. His unique observations and thoughts can bring a smile to your face, a tear to your eye and at times, even surprise you. For anyone looking for real-life, lighthearted, compelling stories, with a touch of humanity and humour, this book delivers!

Paul Shearstone MACP, CCP, NLP
Amazon #1 Best Selling Author, Toronto.

•••••

Konrad has a wonderful descriptive vocabulary allowing him to paint a scene with words and imbue that canvas with just the right kind of emotion and insight.

For readers, Konrad's flowing prose with vivid imagery and pithy dialogue is like a real-time experience, even though he is talking about incidents that happened a while ago. Konrad's writings are always a pleasure to read - and read again!

Bala Menon,
Journalist-Artist-Historian-Author, Toronto.

Introduction

Why isn't the word 'Travelation' in the dictionary?

It describes the travel experience perfectly and would be a fusion of the words travel, revelation and elation.

My wife Jackie and I love to travel. We don't just travel to see the sights but also to observe the different attitudes, values, beliefs and temperaments of people in different places around the world.

Unless you travel you won't know how true Jimmy Buffett's song title

"Changes In Latitudes, Changes In Attitudes" really is.

This book contains personal observations and revelations on how societies in other countries function often in ways that are very different from those that might be considered the norm in our corner of the world.

We were astonished to learn that corruption can be quite useful and simplify life but can also be terribly destructive.

We learned that a good con job could also be considered creative selling and that not taking the law too seriously is in certain circumstances more helpful than having it strictly enforced.

We admired other peoples' solutions to problems that would not be acceptable in Canada but made more sense than our seemingly logical and complicated approach to things that can be solved in a simpler or more creative way.

We often hear the phrase 'thinking outside the box' and found that other cultures practice it much more frequently than we do, often with better results and seldom with disastrous consequences.

These stories are mostly humorous but there are a few that will make you question your sanity or the sanity of the people in those far-away places.

Konrad Brinck,
Toronto, 2019.

❈ Chapter 1

Travelling With Grandchildren

Jackie and I have always loved to be around children, especially when travelling. It is so refreshing to introduce them to new things and see their reactions and express opinions you didn't expect or never thought of yourself.

I have written about my daughter's travels and adventures with us in my memoir 'It's Just Me' and look back at these trips with a smile on my face.

Ivy, our older grandchild, had been to Mexico twice before her sister Kenley arrived. We travelled to Sayulita to spend a week with her when her parents invited us and she visited us as a three year old in the Yucatan a year later.

We had a lot of fun when Ivy and Kenley visited us in our winter home in the Yucatan in 2017 but by far the most memorable trip we've had with them was visiting Germany in 2016.

It was the perfect time to introduce the girls and Toni's spouse Tonya to our relatives in Germany.

My relatives were excited to get to know my Canadian family and went all out to make it a trip for us to remember.

Kenley and Ivy dropped all their shyness and apprehension towards my cousin Gisela and her husband Georg in Ebstorf the moment they explored their property. Their sprawling yard featured a pond stocked with fish, a garden with strawberry beds and fruit to munch on and, most importantly, a tree house to explore and a small 'kiddie cottage' to play in.

It was paradise for them.

Let me first explain how different Kenley and Ivy are.

Ivy is a bookworm who is quite adventurous when it comes to food but less so when it comes to physical challenges like climbing and horsing around.

Kenley was still too young to read but was, and still is, a little daredevil. Her adventurism stops when it comes to food. Fruit, some vegetables, cheese and candy are just about all she loves to eat. She doesn't much care for meat, fish, potatoes or anything new. She is the pickiest eater I've ever seen.

Ivy was so impressed by the meals presented by my cousin that she proclaimed she would open a German restaurant in Canada when she grows up. Even Kenley ate well but mainly because there was always a sweet but healthy option on the table. Waffles with strawberries, blueberries, cream and yogurt made her a happy little girl at the breakfast table.

When it came to being daring, Kenley took the lead. It started on the first day when she climbed up to the top of the tree house. The route down required sliding down a fireman's pole. Kenley could not wait to slide down even though it was a drop of about two and a half meters. We had a hard time making her wait for Georg to get into position in the tree house to make sure she properly gripped the pole and for me to position myself at the bottom to catch her if she fell. She had a broad smile on her face as she slid down and ran for the ladder to climb back up again.

Ivy was not eager to slide down and you could see she was a bit scared but was not going to be upstaged by her little sister.

She didn't have the happiest face coming down and her tense body was clinging to the pole for dear life. With her eyes closed she slid into my arms at the bottom. It took a couple more runs for her to reject Georg's or my help with the descent to the bottom.

We went to many parks and children's playgrounds on this trip and

I noticed that German playgrounds are far more challenging and creative than what we offer children in Canada. There is just as much emphasis on safety as in Canada but German playground designers seem to put much more faith into the abilities of children than we do. There are deep layers of wood chips, rubber pellets or well maintained sandpits to cushion their falls but the challenges are much more daring and varied than what we are used to.

Case in point is a children's village we visited in the Saxony Alps along the river Elbe.

The village had several pint sized replicas of medieval houses representing all kinds of different trades. There was a bakery, a blacksmith, a carpentry, an apothecary and many more. Every building was stocked with real or make-believe items used in these trades for children to play with. Ivy was most interested in the apothecary and made us pretend to have many sicknesses and would mix or recommend herbs and remedies for whatever ailed us.

Kenley was more interested in getting water into a small ditch to get the little watermill going.

There was a tubular, metal climbing scaffold leading to a play house and a large enclosed metal slide about seven meters off the ground. The tube was open all around and acted as a ladder to the top of the slide. It was about ten meters long and led to a slide that promised a steep and fast ride back to terra firma. All of us stood there holding our breath as Kenley made her way up to the tube looking at nothing but the ground below. She managed carefully but without fear or hesitation, not slipping on a single rung, arriving safely at the other side and sliding down to the bottom. There was pride and a definite glimmer of accomplishment in her eyes.

Ivy didn't try it. It was a bit too daunting for her.

I have never seen such a fantastic and imaginative playground in Canada. It was not only fun for the children but for the adults as well.

Ivy is a very observant kid and she became fascinated with the German language.

As we were driving down the Autobahn she suddenly exclaimed that Germans sure do fart a lot. We all just looked at each other and she explained that there are a lot of signs about farting on German roads.

When we asked where she saw signs about farting she pointed at an Exit sign on the side of the road.

Let me explain.

The German word for exit, as far as road signs are concerned, is 'Ausfahrt, and the word for entrance, when entering the Autobahn, is 'Einfahrt'.

We all had a good laugh but if you give a four and a seven year old child a good reason to tell fart jokes, they will never end.

Ivy took in the cultural things Germany had to offer and was thrilled to actually visit castles and fortresses. In Dresden she was quite impressed by the Procession of Princes. This is a large mural of a mounted procession of the rulers of Saxony. It was originally painted between 1871 and 1876 to celebrate the 800th anniversary of the Wettin Dynasty, Saxony's ruling family. In order to make the work weatherproof, it was replaced with approximately 23,000 Meissen porcelain tiles between 1904 and 1907. With a length of 102 metres, it is known as the largest porcelain artwork in the world. The mural displays the ancestral portraits of the many margraves, electors, dukes and kings of the House of Wettin between 1127 and 1904.

Ivy was quite inspired by this massive mural and, thinking of herself as quite an artist, she sat down on the curb and spontaneously started drawing some of the figures.

Before we went to Potsdam and Berlin we actually experienced the highlight of the trip as far as the girls were concerned.

Tropical Islands Resort is a tropical theme park located on a former Airfield 50 kilometres outside of Berlin. It is housed in a former airship hangar, the biggest free-standing hall in the world and is, according to Guinness, the world record holder for the largest indoor waterpark.

We stayed overnight to have two full days of fun. I don't know who had a better time, the adults or the girls.

Jackie and I were definitely more adventurous when it came to our choice of accommodation.

Toni and Tonya chose a hotel room and Jackie and I decided to sleep in a tent in the tropical forest of the resort, right next to the enormous pool with its sandy beach.

I guess the girls would have preferred a night in a tent but their parents insisted on a nice air conditioned room. This was probably the better choice because we didn't realize that the park was kept at a constant 32 degrees Celsius with high humidity. Sleeping in a tent was not very comfortable and we had a tough time falling asleep while continuously wiping the sweat off of our faces.

We woke up early and jumped into the pool to cool down after having a quick shower to wash off the nightsweat.

The girls had a ball. There was no hesitation to try every slide, all the splash pads and river rafts offered.

Both of them still talk about this resort to this day, over two years later.

We left in the late afternoon to continue on to Potsdam for a visit with my relatives.

My cousins live on a farm in a small village just outside of Potsdam called Neu Fahrland. The farm is actually a family compound of many buildings with four generations calling it home.

Wernie and my cousin Ilse live downstairs in the main house. Their grandson Michael and his wife Yvonne and their two children occupy the upstairs living quarters.

Their daughter Bärbel and her husband Manfred were living in the back building which is connected to another house where Wernie's sister lives.

Bärbel's house has two separate apartments where we stayed for our four-day visit.

The farm was a little paradise for the girls. Not only did it have another tree house and lots of animals from giant rabbits to ducks, geese, chickens and little cornish hens but also had a lake at the end of the property with paddleboats and a small sandy beach.

Julius and Jolina, Michael and Yvonne's two children, were thrilled to play, swim and enjoy the things you do on a farm. They took Ivy and Kenley horseback riding and it was amazing how well they got along with their respective lack of English and German. Michael knows a fair bit of English, Yvonne knew a few words, Julius had just started taking English in school and was eager to practice his limited knowledge and at all other times they got by with good old sign language.

We enjoyed our excursions to the palaces and gardens of the Prussian kings in Potsdam. What was most impressive was that they supplied different audio guides for adults and children with age appropriate commentary for the walk through the palace of King Frederick the Great. I don't know what the commentary was for a four year old but Kenley was fascinated by what she heard. Of course it was also great fun for them to slip and slide around in the big felt slippers they give you to wear over your shoes to protect the exquisite parquet floors.

Dinner was always a great affair.

Finally Jackie and I had what we always wanted, a large extended family.

We sat in their beautiful garden and had all the bounty their land and their lake had to offer, fresh smoked eel, fried fish, roasted duck, grilled rabbit, with fresh vegetables and fruit from the garden. Every night the table was brimming with the best food you could imagine.

It certainly gave us and the girls the feeling of being one big family.

All of us had a hard time saying good-bye when we left for Berlin, our last stage of this magnificent trip.

Tonya had rented a spacious three bedroom apartment through Air B&B right in the middle of the city. We had a busy agenda for the next four days.

The days were arranged around sightseeing and the evenings were set aside for adults. Toni and Tonya babysat one night and we stayed home with them the other two nights.

We tried to have as much fun as possible.

Surprisingly the girls enjoyed the sightseeing very much. Ivy was pretty impressed when we visited the Berlin Dome and went into the crypt where she walked past the huge coffins of kings and queens. Ivy was very quiet admiring the monument like sarcophaguses of German nobility of over 500 years. When we got back up to the main church the noon organ concert began. Neither one of the girls had ever experienced the massive sound of a pipe organ inside a church with astounding acoustics.

The German Reichstag, the historic parliament building, was another adventure not only our grandchildren enjoyed. Tonya had arranged for us to have breakfast in the glass dome of the Reichstag.

The large glass dome at the very top of the Reichstag has a 360-degree view of the surrounding Berlin cityscape. The main hall, the debating chamber of the parliament below, can also be seen from inside the dome, and natural light from above radiates down to the parliament floor. A large sun shield tracks the movement of the sun electronically and blocks direct sunlight which would not only cause large solar gain, but dazzle those below. The walk from the top of the dome, along floor to ceiling glass walls showing endless views of the city was spectacular.

I should mention that the breakfast, four omelettes, two children's specials, six juices and three coffees came to almost $150.00 Canadian, making it the most expensive breakfast I've ever had.

It was a park that we visited because of its fairy tale fountain that ended up being the most exciting outing in Berlin. It wasn't memorable because of the many statues of famous German fairytale characters but rather because of its challenging playground.

I don't think either Kenley or Ivy had ever been on a zip line before and it certainly looked like a lot of fun to Kenley but more of a death threat to Ivy.

Kenley again squealed for joy as she was speeding through the air with Ivy looking on. After her sister survived her second run she became a bit more daring and willing to give it a try. Clinging on to the rope with her eyes closed and holding her breath, she zipped along arriving alive and full of bravado at the bottom. From this point on there was no stopping either one of them.

Toni still has a pen-pal from her childhood living in the building where I was born and where she used to visit her grandmother many decades ago.

Putte, as she was called by everybody that knew her, had invited us for afternoon coffee and cake.

She had bought little gifts for the girls and was a gracious host.

However, the big attraction of this visit was that the building is across from the former Tempelhof airport that closed in 2008 and is now a huge open field, park and playground.

People skate, run, cycle and even sailboard on the old runways and Berliners have planted illegal gardens growing vegetables, flowers, bushes and trees. They have even built small garden shacks for storage or shelter. These community gardens are quite a sight and well visited on weekends giving the city dwellers a feeling of being in the open and free from the hustle and bustle of city life.

The time had come to say good-bye to Germany and we did not look forward to our long trek back home.

Getting up at four o'clock in the morning to catch a seven o'clock flight to London, have a five-hour lay over and then board our plane for the eight-hour flight to Toronto was not something we looked forward to.

Ivy and Kenley actually managed better than the adults. They enjoyed a fantastic playground at Heathrow airport and loved the in-flight entertainment. Ivy fell asleep half way through the flight to Toronto but Kenley did not sleep at all.

Jackie asked her why she wouldn't sleep and her answer was a classic;

"Ouma, I really want to sleep but my body won't let me."

It was with the plane starting its descent into Pearson Airport that she was finally overcome with tiredness and fell into a deep sleep and didn't wake up until we had cleared customs, collected our luggage and boarded our separate cabs.

This was one of our most enjoyable trips for everybody involved and left many lasting memories.

I hope to one day take a similar family trip to South Africa to introduce all of them to Jackie's family in one of the most breathtakingly beautiful countries in the world.

❈ Chapter 2

Nightmare Of A Trip Gone Bad

I had planned everything perfectly. What could go wrong?

Our annual winter escape to the South was supposed to be spectacular in 2008.

Jackie and I were looking forward to experiencing some of the more exotic and desirable vacation spots the Americas had to offer.

Starting out on the 25th of January from Fort Lauderdale with a 16 day cruise on Holland America Line's MS Maasdam through the Panama Canal ending up in San Diego where we had planned to stay overnight and fly to Hawaii's Big Island the next day. We and our friends, the Hellens and the Spiers, had rented a three-bedroom townhouse in Waikoloa Beach Resort for two weeks. The condo was overlooking the beach and we would be there for the whale watching season. The owner had told me that we could watch them right from our patio.

Jackie and I would fly back to San Diego after our stay in this Hawaiian paradise to spend two more weeks in a beachfront condo in Oceanside, California. We had vacationed there before and loved it. The complex offered amenities like swimming pools, lush gardens, shopping, dining and a golf course. Just a stone's throw away from our place was a quaint harbour with craft, candy and antique shops giving it a small town flavour of days gone by.

We still planned a week-long trip to Las Vegas and had arranged to drop our rental car off at the airport to fly home.

I had taken great care to purchase travel health insurance and cancellation insurance for our flight itinerary San Diego - Hawaii - San Diego - Las Vegas -Toronto and had purchased separate cancellation insurance for the cruise directly from Holland America Cruise Lines.

We were all set. What could go wrong?

Everything!

It was a glorious day as we pulled out of Fort Lauderdale. A steward served special welcome cocktails as we stood on the Lido Deck watching the harbour slowly disappear on the horizon and listening to a dance band playing popular tunes to put us in a holiday mood.

The next two days at sea were spent soaking up the sunshine lying by the swimming pool while sipping delicious cocktails. We indulged in the culinary delights prepared by an outstanding collection of chefs on board ship. The entertainment offered every night at the theatre which included international artists like Frankie Avalon as well as dancers, comedians and magicians that could have easily been part of any Las Vegas show, was a fitting way to end the day.

Even though the bar stayed open until well after midnight with a band playing to keep the younger crowd dancing, we opted to get a good night's sleep.

When we reached our first port of call, Cartagena, Colombia, we took an excursion to get to know this fascinating city and its citizens and were not disappointed.

After a day at sea we finally arrived at the Panama Canal.

It was everything we had expected. A marvel of engineering that left us breathless as we passed through locks pulled by huge trollies and we were in awe of the crew's skill to get us through the narrow channels without damaging the ship.

After another day at sea we arrived at Puntarenas, Costa Rica. Jackie and I had just been to Costa Rica the previous year on a month-long vacation and had seen all the sights that Holland America was offering for their shore excursions and decided to explore the city ourselves and do some souvenir shopping.

If we had stayed on board ship, gone to the beach or taken one of the ecological tours, my life would not have been in chaos for the next eight months.

A simple little moment of not paying attention was about to almost kill me in a painful and unexpected way and make my life a living hell.

Our souvenir shopping was done and we were standing on a street corner looking around to see if we should try to find another bargain or go back to the ship.

We decided to have a drink at a small restaurant across the street and without looking I stepped off the sidewalk. My left foot went straight down into a partially covered sewer.

The opening was just big enough for my leg to sink deeper and deeper without touching ground. I felt almost like being in a dream where you fall helplessly into an abyss. The momentum of my step made my body go forward and my shin scraped along the opening of the grade scratching the flesh and skin of my shin.

Falling forward without being able to get my leg out of the sewer I thought I'd break it but was able to bend forward and cushion the fall with my hands. My left leg was now wedged into the sewer and the right one was totally bent which made me tilt over to the left.

Jackie was terrified as she saw my leg disappear. She dropped our parcels and tried to catch me.

Her shrieking outcry got the attention of some passersby who came to my aid.

I think it was the adrenalin rush that kept me from panicking and from feeling any pain on my leg. It was only after two strong men pulled me out of my predicament that I felt pain in my hyper-extended knee and the burning sensation of having my skin and flesh scraped off of my shinbone.

The bleeding went from a trickle to a flood in seconds. The blood ran down into my socks and running shoes. My leg was covered in the muddy substance that was caked on the sidewalls of the sewer.

Luckily there was a drugstore right across the street. The pharmacist cleaned me up and put some disinfectant on the wound. After he had bandaged my leg he told me to get back to the ship to have the ship doctor apply further treatment since he had a tough time trying to stop the bleeding.

The pain in my knee had subsided slightly as I hobbled back to the ship without too much of a problem.

The doctor's office was only open from 7:00 to 9:00 am, and opened again from 5:00 to 7:00 pm after the ship had left port. We had to wait a while for the doctor to show up. Cruise ship doctors are poorly paid and sign up to have a vacation interrupted by a few hours of work in the morning and evening.

Dr Holtzman was not the friendliest physician I've ever met but he knew what he was doing in the grumpiest way possible. I felt I was guilty of interfering with his holiday plans and he was trying to get rid of me as fast as possible. After I told him what had happened he cleaned the scrapes thoroughly and used Steri-Strips to hold my skin together.

He then ordered me to stay out of the pool for three to four days and said I would be fine after that.

I paid my bill of $86.26 US and Jackie and I thought we could put this little episode behind us. At least we had a good story to tell at our always enjoyable dinner that night.

I had a couple of extra Cognacs before bed to calm my nerves and dull the slight pain I was still experiencing.

The next morning my leg had turned black and blue and was hurting quite a bit. I was not very concerned thinking that there must be a deep-seated bruise after the punishment my leg took the day before. I decided to follow the doctor's orders and stay in bed all day to rest my battered body.

That evening we did go out for dinner even though I noticed that the wound was oozing some clear liquid and my calf muscle started to hurt.

The following morning the pain was excruciating. The oozing was now mixed with what looked like pus and I was running a slight fever.

Jackie urged me to go and see the doctor but when we got there just five minutes after nine o'clock his office was already closed. I had to wait until the evening.

We were back before five o'clock and waiting for his office door to open. When Dr Holtzman looked at my leg he stared at me and said, "Why didn't you come earlier to see me?"

I had never heard the term 'Necrotizing Fasciitis' and didn't really know what it was. Since the doctor was busy yelling at his nurse to get him medication and fresh bandages I didn't ask him to give me a detailed explanation of what necrotizing fasciitis was. The doctor injected me with some antibiotics, gave me a pain killer and told me we would have to disembark in the morning to get me into a hospital since the flesh around my shin would have to be surgically removed.

I asked him if it was possible to rejoin the ship after the surgery and he just looked at me and said that this was highly unlikely.

"Okay," I said, "what about a day or two later? I have a plane to catch in San Diego to continue my vacation in Hawaii."

Smiling at me, he said that it was a decision the surgeon had to make, he couldn't say.

He told me not to worry about a thing. He would call my travel insurance company and arrange for an ambulance and a hospital in Acapulco which was our next port of call. He gave me a wheelchair and instructed me to lie down and get some rest and not to eat anything after midnight.

He charged me another $191.34 US and told us to be back in his office at 6:00 am the next morning for a final treatment and consultation with the Mexican doctor.

After I ate my dinner in the cabin I felt a bit better and, since Jackie was busy packing, I decided to wheel myself to the Internet-cafe to send an email to my friends telling them I had a bit of a health problem and was still hoping to get to Hawaii in time.

When Dr. Holtzman saw me rolling down the aisle he came up to me and said: "Didn't I tell you to stay in bed? You have no idea how sick you are. Get back to your cabin immediately."

The way he said it made me feel worried for the first time.

Early the next morning the cabin steward came to pick up our luggage and Jackie wheeled me to the doctor's office.

Dr Holtzman gave me another injection and charged another $166.00 US to my final bill for the consultation.

The purser handed me my final bill and said they had already put it on my Visa account. He then handed me the receipt and the statement for a short but unforgettable cruise on Holland America Cruise Lines.

A Mexican doctor and two orderlies boarded the ship to have a look at me. The doctor introduced himself as Dr Mario Campuzano, the head surgeon of the Hospital Santa Lucia, a private hospital in Acapulco.

Dr Holtzman and Dr Campuzano exchanged a few words and I was put on a gurney and taken off the ship with customs and immigration officers standing at the gangway to check and stamp our passports.

I was loaded into an ambulance and 15 minutes later arrived at the hospital. Dr Campuzano made me fill out an admission form and an authorization to go ahead with the operation.

He also asked for my credit card and explained that the insurance company would repay me but he would put my final bill on my credit card. To reassure me he showed me a fax from the insurance confirming that I was covered under the terms of my policy.

He also explained what necrotizing fasciitis was. That was the first time I heard that I had 'Flesh Eating Disease'.

I was shocked.

Dr Campuzano explained that he thought they may have caught it in time but if I had waited one more day I would most likely have died or at least lost my leg.

With that an orderly rolled me into the operating theatre and two minutes later the anaesthesiologist told me to count backwards from 99 to zero.

When I opened my eyes again I saw Jackie staring at me with a worried look on her face.

She was holding my hand as she asked me if I was okay.

"I feel fine," I replied trying to smile.

Dr Campuzano was standing at the foot of the bed holding a chart.

He looked at me and said, "You are one lucky man. We had to cut quite a lot of your soft tissue away but you are going to be fine. We saved your leg but it will take a long time to heal."

"So we won't be able to go on to Hawaii?" I asked, hoping not to get a 'no' for an answer.

"You will need a lot of care and we will try to get you in good enough shape to get you back to Canada where you will need to see a doctor right away to get further treatment and care."

It finally sank in that this trip was over.

"How long will I have to stay here?" I asked.

"If everything goes as planned you should be able to fly home in three to five days," he said and continued telling us that they would try to make our stay as comfortable as possible.

Jackie told me she could stay with me in the room, pointing to a pullout couch across the room. I was glad to hear that. Having to be alone while Jackie stayed in a hotel would have been hard on both of us.

As we were talking a woman walked into the room and Dr Campuzano introduced her to us as Carmen Hudson.

She was our concierge and we could call her 24 hours a day. Her English was perfect but she had a slight Spanish accent. She had married an American who lived in Mexico and ran an import/export business in Acapulco.

She explained that her duty was to keep us happy and she would try to arrange anything we wanted. Carmen gave us her cell phone number and told us we could call her at any time of the day.

She would take Jackie shopping or sightseeing, order special meals, anything from McDonald's to gourmet dinners, if we didn't like the hospital food and make the travel arrangements back to Toronto when I would be ready to be released.

I was impressed. This kind of service and patient care was certainly not available in Canada.

I looked around and noticed that this room looked more like a living room with a hospital bed in it than a traditional sterile hospital room back home.

There was a wall unit with a big 30" TV in it, the aforementioned sofa and an armchair with a coffee table, a closet to store our suitcases and to hang up Jackie's clothes. The outside wall had a huge panoramic window overlooking Acapulco Bay.

This was more like a luxury hotel room than a hospital room.

We thanked Carmen and told her we would call if we needed her but she said she'd be back in the morning to plan the day for Jackie to possibly explore Acapulco with her.

Dr Campuzano said he'd be back that night to change my dressing and keep an eye on my wound.

I still felt weak and dozed off after everybody had left.

Jackie was watching TV when I woke up late in the afternoon. We had a good cable package offering many American and Spanish stations.

There was a large tray with snacks, fruits and juices on my bedside table. I was starved. I had not eaten since the previous evening and devoured everything on the tray.

A delicious dinner arrived shortly after and Jackie and I had our first conversation in a couple of days. Jackie was still worried about my health and about getting me safely home. I was more disappointed that this marvellous trip had ended in disaster.

After dinner Dr Campuzano arrived to change my dressing.

When he removed the bandages I saw my leg, or what was left of it, for the first time.

There was no flesh. I could see my shin bone and my calf muscle. My leg looked like one of these anatomical pictures in medical books, only more bloody and unappetizing.

Jackie turned away in horror and I had a tough time imagining that this could ever look normal again.

The next morning I remembered that I had to call the travel insurance company to let them know that I had to forfeit my flights and would need to collect on my cancellation insurance.

Carmen was kind enough to put a collect call through to RBC Insurance in Canada.

I explained my situation to the agent of RBC and she informed me she would start a file on me but I would have to contact the airlines and try to negotiate a re-booking or ask for a full or partial refund. The airline then would have to fax or email me their offer or refusal and I could ask them to send a copy to RBC Insurance or forward the answer myself to their office before my first flight was scheduled to depart.

I first thought the claims adjuster on the other end didn't understand my situation or was not familiar with the kind of ticket we had purchased.

"You don't seem to understand," I said. "It says right on my tickets that they are non-refundable and non-cancellable. I can have the tickets faxed to you this afternoon"

"Sir," she replied in a rather condescending voice, "if you read your policy you will see that it clearly states that you have to make an effort to negotiate a refund or ask to have your flights changed. Airlines quite often make exceptions and if you refuse to do that then we will not allow your claim."

"Lady," I said, trying to again explain my circumstances, " I am in Mexico in a hospital bed with half my leg missing due to flesh eating disease and don't have the energy, nor the means, to look up telephone numbers of airlines and beg for concessions I am not entitled to."

"Well sir," she retorted in the same snotty way she had talked to me before, "you were aware of the terms of the policy and all we are asking is that you adhere to them."

It took quite a bit of self-control not to swear and scream at her. I asked for her name and direct number and told her that I, or somebody on my behalf, would be in touch with her.

Luckily I had booked the flights through the Flight Centre, a large travel agency. I called Shannon, the travel agent we had used for many years, to tell her about the predicament I was in and asked if she could contact the airlines and get a fax to RBC so we would not lose out on collecting for our missed flights. Shannon assured me that she would look after everything and not to worry as she had done this before and knew how to handle the situation.

For the first time I was glad that I didn't book my flights and buy insurance over the internet. This taught me the value of having contact with a human being that still knows how to look after a customer instead of a website that only knows you by your IP address.

The rest of the day was pretty uneventful. I slept a lot while Jackie and Carmen went shopping for the afternoon.

Dr Campuzano dropped in that evening and informed me that he would be back in the morning to have another look at my leg to see if they had cut away all of the infected flesh. If everything was clear I could make arrangements with Carmen to go home the following day.

Early in the morning he returned with, what he called a specialist in necrotizing fasciitis, who noticed signs of bacterial growth and they determined that some more surgery was needed.

Shortly after lunch I was wheeled back into the OR and was again put under to lose some more flesh from my left leg. I wondered if there would be any left when I awoke again.

Jackie was holding my hand again as I opened my eyes and looked less worried than just 48 hours earlier. Dr Campuzano told me they were confident that all of the infected areas had been removed and I was ready to go home after another day of observation and recuperation. In the morning he would give Carmen the green light to book our flight home and make arrangements to get me to the airport.

He and Carmen showed up very early the next day.

Dr Campuzano removed the dressing and marvelled at his surgical masterpiece, or the remnants of my once perfect leg.

Jackie couldn't bear to look and turned away. Actually I don't think she looked at it for the next few months. It was not a pretty sight.

The green light was given and Dr Campuzano promised to come back that evening to give me final instructions and say good bye to us since we would catch the early flight to Mexico City at 6:00 am and would have to leave the hospital not later than four o'clock in the morning.

As promised he came to see us and brought his whole family along. He wanted them to meet Jackie and me since he had told them so much about our plans, the shattered dreams of a fabulous journey and the way we handled our misfortune.

After he explained to me that I should check into a hospital as soon as I arrived in Toronto and give the attending physician the folder with my files to let them decide on further treatments.

I was handed extra-strength painkillers and an instruction sheet with the Do's and Don'ts while in transit. Carmen handed us our plane tickets and told me that the airlines were informed about my special needs and would make special arrangements for wheelchairs, boarding, seating etc.

We all kissed and hugged like old friends saying good-bye to each other knowing that we most likely would never see each other again.

It was still dark the next morning when I was taken downstairs and put into a special wheelchair-equipped cab to start my long journey home.

The flight to Toronto was pretty uneventful. We had a three-hour layover in Mexico City but the service awarded to me to make my flight a pleasant experience was excellent. The only problem came when nature called.

I was given strictest orders to keep my leg elevated at all times if possible. I boarded the plane in my wheelchair but there was none available during the flight. Even though we were seated at the bulkhead, the journey to the lavatory was a challenge and keeping my leg elevated while I was conducting my business was impossible unless I kept the toilet door open, an option that did not appeal to me. Somehow I managed, but I experienced a considerable amount of pain for the first time since the operation.

Our friend Susan was waiting for us at the airport to take me to a hospital.

We first went home to drop off the luggage and change into some winter clothes.

We decided that we would go to the emergency department of Toronto General Hospital assuming that it would be best equipped to handle anything including flesh eating disease.

To everybody's surprise the waiting room was almost empty and I was attended to right away.

Jackie handed the triage nurse the folder given to us and when she read the words necrotizing fasciitis she pulled a disgusting face and told me to hold on for just a minute.

Five minutes later they pushed me into the examination room and a young doctor removed the bandages, had one good look at my now dried up, discoloured wound and said the words that sent shivers down my spine: "Oh my god, that looks terrible! I think we'll have to amputate."

I was shocked. I can't remember the thoughts that went through my mind but I was utterly speechless and it took me a few moments to say,

"The doctors in Mexico said they got it all and I would be okay. Are you sure you'll have to amputate?"

"Well," he answered," we will have to call in a specialist from Toronto Western Hospital. They normally handle these types of cases and have a whole team to handle bacterial infections and things like gangrene and necrotizing fasciitis that call for amputations. I'll ask them to come over and have a look."

They left me in my little cubicle for the next two hours. Those were most likely the longest two hours of my life, with images of people on crutches, one-legged, disabled and paraplegic athletes trying to participate in sports tailored to people without limbs going through my mind like a horror movie.

Jackie and Susan tried to talk me into being positive and wait for the second opinion of the specialists. It was hard for me to do that.

Two doctors arrived from Toronto Western to examine me further. They were joined by a specialist from Toronto General who had just been appointed to head the unit to look after cases like mine.

They poked, smelled, scraped and pulled my leg and after about ten minutes the older doctor from Toronto Western said, "We will have to run a few more tests but everything looks okay to me. You will need lots of treatment and special care but you will be okay."

"So no amputation?" I hesitantly enquired and looked at him with great anticipation.

"Absolutely not," he said smiling at me. "Those doctors in Mexico did a fantastic job. You are a very lucky man. My colleague's diagnosis was a bit hasty. I guess he hasn't seen too many wounds like yours before and necrotizing fasciitis is not a common occurrence in the ER."

The doctor from Toronto General introduced herself to me as Dr Joan Lipa and told me that she would be the one looking after me from then on.

I immediately liked her whole personality and caring demeanour. I knew I was in good hands. Her first priority was to get me admitted and find me a bed because at that point there were none available on her floor.

The next 36 hours were not a fun time. I was literally left in a supply closet in the emergency department. The closet was so small that my gurney prevented the door from being shut which meant I had no privacy. No TV or telephone was available until I was moved to a proper room. At least I had a lot of visitors in the morning when housekeeping came around to stock up on supplies.

I must say that everybody tried very hard to make me as comfortable as possible and supply me with everything I asked for.

On the second day I was told that a bed had become available and I would be moved that afternoon. It was nice to experience the last bit of sunshine and be in a room with a window, my own bathroom, a telephone and a television set.

It wasn't as luxurious as my room in Mexico but it certainly was a relief to be out of the closet.

This would now become my home for the next two weeks.

Dr Lipa took a special interest in me and told me the next day that they would try a fairly new treatment on me called Negative-pressure wound therapy (NPWT). This is a therapeutic technique using a vacuum dressing to promote healing of acute or chronic wounds. The therapy involves the controlled application of sub-atmospheric pressure to the local wound environment using a sealed wound dressing connected to a vacuum pump. She said this treatment, even though still experimental, had shown great promise in regrowing tissue.

The machine arrived a couple of days later and I was told that a portable unit would be ordered for home use once I was released from hospital.

It was kind of awkward to have to pull a machine around and having my mobility restricted to the length of the extension cord but I got used to it. Every day I was disconnected for a couple of hours to use the internet on the floor, have a shower and enjoy a bit of freedom to hobble or roll around in my wheelchair.

I also used my time to contact the insurance companies to make sure my claims were processed and I would be properly reimbursed for my flights and my medical expenses that were in excess of $20,000.00. Both insurance companies told me not to worry since I had 90 days to get my claims documented and both, RBC for my flight cancellation and Medipac for my health insurance, needed more release forms signed to access my medical records from the cruise line, the Mexican hospital and from OHIP. They would send them to my home and I could sign and return them at my earliest convenience.

The days went by fairly quickly. I had lots of visitors, friendly nurses and lots of books and a great cable package for my television viewing pleasure.

As usual, even though at times acceptable, the food needed to be supplemented with something edible, so every visitor who asked me if they could bring me something the answer was always 'yes'. The requests ranged from a good hamburger to a delicious Subway sandwich with lots of hot peppers.

After two weeks Dr Lipa said that my progress was good enough for me to be released in a few days and she would go ahead and order home care for me. She also signed a request for a 'handicapped' parking sticker for six months since I would have to use crutches for an extended period of time.

Once all the supplies, a portable vacuum machine and daily nursing visits were arranged I was ready to be discharged.

Two days later my friend Horst came to pick me up.

It was good to be home again. Jackie was all smiles and had made one of her great curry dishes to welcome me and give me everything I had been craving; a homecooked spicy meal, a hug, a welcome kiss and my own bed.

Our living room was stacked with all kinds of medical supplies including a pair of crutches.

The vacuum pump was supposed to arrive the next morning and the nurse called to make the initial appointment to change my dressing and train me on how to use the machine.

The doorbell woke me up the next morning and Jackie went downstairs to answer it. It was the delivery of my vacuum pump. The nurse was only coming at 10:00 am but I was curious to see the instructions, the size and the weight of this gadget that I had to carry around with me for the next three months. It was smaller than I thought, just about the size of a small shoe box weighing less than four pounds and the manual said I had to keep it plugged in whenever an outlet was available. Unplugged, it could run for three to four hours on its built-in batteries. It would, however, take up to eight hours to recharge if completely drained of power. It came with a nice leatherette carrying case that I could sling over my shoulder when I was going out.

The nurse arrived right on time and introduced herself as Joan. She was going to care for me as long as she was needed. For the first little while she would change the dressing daily, then every second day and close to the end only every third day.

Joan had a great sense of humour and we never had a problem finding things to talk about for the 30 minutes she spent with me.

At home I hung the unit from an intravenous stand and pushed it around. There was only about three meters of tubing running from the dressing up my pant leg into the machine which did not give me a lot of room to move without having to drag the pump along.

For the first few weeks I was not supposed to put too much weight on my leg and use the crutches when moving about. It took me a while to learn how to use the crutches and carry the pump over my shoulder at the same time but I managed pretty well after a bit of practice.

When I felt confident with my crutches and getting around safely without falling, my priority was getting the papers to the insurance companies.

My first trip was to RBC for my flight cancellation claim. Their offices were only ten minutes away and I drove there for my appointment with Ms Fersey Rajan, my insurance adjuster, who took my papers, the signed forms and plane tickets.

Ms Rajan said she would process them and that everything looked to be in order. I talked to her about the efforts by my travel agent, who contacted the airlines and wrote letters and faxes and asked her if they would have denied my claim if my travel agent wouldn't have gotten involved while I was bedridden.

She simply replied that they were only enforcing the terms of the policy and didn't want to discuss it any further. I didn't want to push the issue and tell her how insensitive and uncooperative the person was that I dealt with from my hospital bed in Mexico.

Ms Rajan assured me the claim, if everything checked out, would be settled within four to six weeks and a check would be mailed to me.

I hobbled back to my car and drove home being proud of myself for having completed my first outing on crutches with my steady companion, the vacuum pump.

The next day I had made an appointment with my claims adjuster Michael McNeil from MEDIPAC at his office in Don Mills. He had said I could just mail all my papers in but I insisted on coming in person since I wanted to answer any questions he may have had in order to expedite my claim.

I mentioned I would only have 90 minutes to spend with him since it would take me 45 minutes each way travel time and my pump was only good for three to four hours without being plugged into a wall socket. He assured me we would only be 20 minutes at the most to go over the forms and I would be on my way.

Mr McNeil seemed like a nice man and made a great effort to make me feel comfortable and showed a lot of empathy for the situation I was in. He offered me a cup of coffee and, as promised we were finished in less than 20 minutes.

It was in early April, after I had inquired about the status of my claim with both insurance companies, that I received a letter from each company on the same day.

RBC sent a check for $1882.00, the full amount I had claimed, thanked me for my business and declared the matter closed.

MEDIPAC sent me a letter informing me that my claim had been denied. I was ineligible due to the fact that I had lied on the application and was not entitled to the policy that I had purchased.

I was stunned, befuddled, furious and ready to fight their decision.

Their decision to deny my claim was based on two questions which were:

1. Have you ever been diagnosed with heart disease?
2. Are you taking any medication or have you ever been prescribed medication to treat your heart disease?

The reason for me answering no to both questions is a long story and started in December of 2006.

I was shocked to receive a phone call from my friend Horst's daughter Michelle that her father had a heart attack and had been taken to the hospital by ambulance. Even though Horst was a smoker he seemed to be in good shape had a physically demanding job and had never complained about any chest pains.

Horst survived his but when a former colleague of mine died of a massive one just a few weeks later I thought I'd better make sure that my own heart was healthy.

I had been smoking for over forty years, was overweight and not exactly in the best shape of my life.

At my next physical check-up with my family doctor, Dr Tautkus, I asked him to give me a referral to a cardiologist to have a stress test and an ECG done since I wanted a clean bill of health for my three months winter get-away in Mexico.

I was referred to Dr Jeejeebhoy who performed the aforementioned tests and an ultrasound after the stress test showed a slight irregularity.

Dr Jeejeebhoy said that it was most likely something minor but just to make sure she arranged a nuclear CT scan.

The result was once again inconclusive.

She said she would put in a request for an angiogram at the Toronto General Hospital but it had to wait until I came back from Mexico since there is a four- to six-week waiting period for non-urgent cases.

She prescribed Metoprolol, a beta-blocker for 'therapeutic' reasons and advised me to carry nitro spray to be on the safe side.

When I filled out my forms for the travel insurance I had no idea on how to answer the two aforementioned questions. I called MEDIPAC and spoke to somebody explaining that I had tests but that they were inconclusive and I didn't know if I was suffering from a heart condition.

I was advised to talk to my cardiologist and answer according to her advice.

Dr Jeejeebhoy assured me that I don't have heart disease and to answer 'No' to both questions since the Metroprolol was only prescribed for therapeutic and precautionary reasons.

I was approved for my policy, paid the premium of $678.40, and assumed to be insured for any medical emergency.

I was wrong.

Jackie had to calm me down and we decided to call Michael McNeil to argue my case.

I tried to be very unemotional when he answered the phone.

"Mr McNeil," I said, trying to sound relaxed and reasonable, "I received your letter and think that you don't have all the facts. I called your company and asked somebody in your underwriting department what my answer to the question about heart conditions should be since I was never given a diagnosis or had a conclusive test result.

"I was told that I should talk to my doctor and mark the questions accordingly. That's exactly what I did. Since you are recording all your phone calls I ask you to check your records to verify my story."

"Can you have your doctor confirm this in a letter to us?" he asked.

"Of course," I replied and asked him if he would reconsider their ruling and accept my claim if Dr Jeejeebhoy confirmed my story.

"We will see what she says and might have another look at it," he said trying to sound non-committal.

It took me almost two weeks to see Dr Jeejeebhoy. She was shocked about MEDIPAC's decision and promised to write a letter immediately.

She said that her brother was a lawyer specializing in insurance law and to give him a call if I should run into further trouble.

I thanked her for the all the help she had given me and hoped that her letter would settle the matter without me having to hire a lawyer.

I called Mr McNeil the following week and he acknowledged receiving the letter from my cardiologist.

"So then you will honor my claim?" I asked.

"Oh no," he said. "We haven't changed our mind at all. We are still denying your claim."

"Why?" I said, "She confirmed my story, didn't she?"

"Oh yes," he retorted, "but we disagree with your doctor's diagnosis."

I was speechless and felt anger building up inside me.

"I don't give a fuck if you disagree with my doctor," I yelled into the phone, losing my composure, "you take it up with my doctor not me. I did what you told me to do."

"Well," he said, annoying and enraging me even further, "you didn't disclose that you were prescribed Metoprolol when asked on the application."

"I was told that I was supposed to take Metoprolol for therapeutic reasons and to prevent heart disease, not to treat it," I replied.

He informed me that he could not find any references to Metoprolol as a therapeutic or preventative drug and would stand by his decision. I told him that I would get legal advice and that this matter was not closed yet as far as I was concerned.

I also told him that my doctor told me that an insurance company cannot, under Ontario law, refuse paying a bill that is covered by the terms of the policy.

I hung up on him when he said, "Oh yes we can. We are not OHIP. The 'Out Of Country Insurance Industry' is an unregulated industry and we can do whatever we want to!"

I felt like I was fighting windmills that were trying to wear me out by intimidating me. I contacted Dr Jeejeebhoy to ask her for her brother's telephone number and she gave me his private line at his law firm of Stanley, Tick and Associates.

He was very helpful but told me that suing would not be an option he would advise me to take.

My claim was less than $20,000.00 and part of that could be recovered claiming it through OHIP, which would leave me with a sum of approximately $17,000.00.

Going to fight it in court would cost between $40,000.00 and $60,000.00 and even if I won I might not get my costs reimbursed.

I felt resignation and defeat taking over and contemplated giving up.

"However," he continued after a short pause, "we do have an Insurance Ombudsman in Ontario and it is exactly these kinds of cases he would look into."

He urged me to notify MEDIPAC that I will take this matter to the Ontario Ombudsman and see how they respond to my complaint.

He also asked me to copy him in on any correspondence and stay in touch and contact him if I needed further advice. He said it always helps to copy a reputable law firm into any correspondence so the other party is aware that you mean business.

I asked how much he would charge me and he said in this case his advice was free as long as he didn't have to do any actual work. He added that he was glad to help one of his sister's patients.

I called Mr McNeil and told him that I was taking this matter to the Ontario Ombudsman.

"That's fine," he answered and then surprised me by saying, "If you want to I can present your case to an independent review board established by Manulife Financial and other institutions that is advising the industry on disputes like this. Would you be willing to have your case reviewed by them?"

I gave it some thought and agreed under one condition, that I could outline my side of the story.

He agreed and I started to write a letter that he would submit to the review board, with every detail about my encounters with MEDIPAC from the application to the denial of my claim. I also repeated all my doctor's advice, diagnoses and explanations.

I did not mention that I had obtained legal counsel but copied the law firm of Mr. Jeejeebhoy in on the bottom of the letter.

On July 17th, a month later, I received a reply from a Barbara Jin of Manulife acknowledging the receipt of my letter and informing me that she would contact me again after the completion of their review.

On August 15th, I received the verdict from Manulife.

I opened the envelope with bated breath.

Ms Jin started by recapping all the events, especially Dr Jeejeebhoy's medical notes and my answers to the relevant questions.

She noted that I had been prescribed a beta-blocker, aspirin and nitro-spray by my cardiologist and that Dr Jeejeebhoy told me that I do not have heart disease, all tests had been inconclusive and the medications were therapeutic and preventative.

However, she continued by saying, and I quote: "Mr. Brinck, the question on the medical questionnaire/application asks if in the 12 months prior you were prescribed or had taken 2 or more oral medications for diabetes and a heart condition. It does not ask if you were prescribed 2 or more oral medications for diabetes and heart disease. You were prescribed Metroprolol, Nitrospray and Aspirin by a cardiologist for a presumed heart condition. As such, the above noted question required an affirmative response."

At this point my hope of having my claim approved evaporated, as it seemed they were going to split hairs about 'heart condition' versus 'heart disease' in their argument against me.

To my surprise the next sentence in her report turned my fortunes around: "However, as the nuclear testing and CT angiogram results were inconclusive, we have proceeded to approve your claim on an ex-gratia basis. Payment of your expenses incurred as the result of your medical emergency is not an admission of liability and Manulife Financial reserves the right to enforce all terms, conditions and provisions of the policy."

Did I win? Did they say they had approved my claim but then said they were not liable?

TRAV-EL-ATIONS

As I turned to the next page there it was.

A cheque for $17,467.00......Hallelujah!

A little disclaimer stated that by signing and cashing the cheque I do acknowledge that there was no liability by Manulife and they, to paraphrase, would pay the money out of the goodness of their hearts.

At that point I really didn't care and understood that they were just covering their ass so this could not be used as a precedent.

It felt so good to have won a battle against a giant corporation.

Jackie and I went out to celebrate that night and I must say.........

Dom Pérignon never tasted so good.

KONRAD BRINCK

❋ Chapter 3

Bait And Switch In Bali

Bali is a beautiful island and delivers everything its tourist industry promises. One fact never mentioned in Bali's travel brochures is poverty. There is no visible poverty close to the luxurious resorts nor is there a high crime rate on this picturesque island.

As a tourist you feel safe and are surrounded by astonishing beauty and people dressed in colourful, traditional clothing.

It is close to tourist attractions, like temples, restaurants and markets where one is bombarded with the most aggressive beggars and sellers of trinkets you can imagine.

The most disturbing thing is that the majority of vendors and beggars are children. At one holy site I was swarmed by a group of boys, none older than ten years.

I literally had to fight them off and, at one point, I felt somebody reaching into my pants pocket. I turned abruptly and yelled at a boy, whose hand I ripped out of my pocket assuming he was a pickpocket, to get away from me.

He stared at me and reached out with his empty hand and said; "You owe me money for flower."

"I owe you nothing, get away from me." I yelled back, getting extremely annoyed.

"Sir, check your pocket," he replied. I reached into my trouser pocket and felt something very soft and pulled out a beautiful jasmine flower. The sweet aroma hit my nose instantly and as I looked into his soft eyes he smiled at me with an expression of desperation and anticipation of a small donation.

My anger subsided and I reluctantly gave him the equivalent of a quarter and his eyes lit up immediately. He thanked me in a polite and gracious manner and ran away.

Other children saw what happened and swarmed me again expecting more generous donations assuming they'd found a rich and giving tourist.

I yelled and flailed my arms around to fight them off and finally went on my way to a sacred waterfall in a gorgeous setting.

On our way, along the side of the well manicured path, some local vendors were selling their wares in a more subdued non-aggressive manner.

A young well-dressed girl, about three years old, was standing on a small platform, all by herself, with little bracelets hanging over her outstretched arm yelling in a soft monotone voice, "One dollar, one dollar."

She looked so cute in her native dress with her long black hair and we started to wonder if we shouldn't spend a dollar to make her happy.

We debated the wrongs and rights of supporting the exploitation of children and the uncaring attitude of her parents who let her stand there all by herself for hours on end without the protection of an adult.

We considered the pros and cons but decided to buy one of her bracelets on our way back from the waterfall. In a way it would make us feel better to see a little girl happy and knowing her family had enough money to buy food that night.

We spotted her, still standing there, half yelling and half whispering "One dollar, one dollar', at the passing tourists.

I went over to this cute, innocent-looking doll and said, "Let me see what you've got."

She stretched out her arm towards me and showed me her collection of bracelets. They were all the same, beads on a rubber band about twenty centimetres long in different colours. To make it more exciting I asked my wife Jackie to choose one.

She pointed to a red and white coloured bracelet.

Immediately the little girl said, in a loud and commanding voice: "That one two dollars!"

I hate it when I get so rattled that I lose my self control but I looked at her in disbelief and said, "Oh fuck off!"

She was barely out of diapers and already an accomplished con artist but was much too cute and adorable to stay mad at.

I just gave her the dollar and took the bracelet. I mumbled an apology for my outburst but was convinced she didn't understand any English beyond the two phrases 'One dollar' and 'That one two dollars'.

We had a good little laugh about the brazen sales tactics of a three year-old on our way to the bus.

I am glad that I can't even imagine a situation like that in Canada.

We can thank our child labour laws, numerous Children's Aid Societies and an extensive welfare system for keeping our children from begging and hawking trinkets on the streets of Canadian cities.

Chapter 4

Getting Shot In Mexico

It was 2002 and not everybody had a cell phone. Long-distance cards were very popular to stay in touch with your loved ones when travelling. Skype was not introduced until later that year.

We spent our first year as snowbirds in Mexico that year in the little fishing village of Chicxulub. There was one internet cafe and one telephone booth to keep in touch with the outside world.

Our friends Erwin and Beate had rented an apartment in the same building as we did.

Chicxulub was and still is a peaceful place where nothing much happens. The inhabitants are mainly fishermen and tradespeople but a few also engage in hunting to support their families.

One evening Erwin decided to call his daughter back home in Canada and went to the telephone booth to make the call.

He noticed some children were playing on a flat roof close to the telephone and it looked like they were playing with a gun. Erwin assumed it was a realistic looking toy gun and didn't pay much attention to them.

In the middle of his conversation he heard a pop followed by a stinging pain in his left calf.

"I think I have been shot," he said to his daughter. "I've got to get to a doctor. Don't worry, I think it is just a flesh wound."

It turned out the kids, about ten or twelve years old, were target-shooting and one bullet went through a neighbouring thatched roof, ricocheted off a beam and hit Erwin's leg.

He was still able to walk to a drugstore just a block away where the pharmacist put a light dressing on the wound and sent him off to the little country hospital in Chicxulub. There the doctor assessed the injury and the nurse cleaned and bandaged the leg properly.

The police (really just one officer) arrived while Erwin was being treated. He had been called by a neighbour who witnessed the incident. While Erwin was treated the officer asked him what had happened and Erwin told him that he had observed the two boys target-shooting on the roof but assumed it was a toy or BB gun.

After he was all stitched up the officer took him back to the scene of the crime.

The boys had long since disappeared. The friendly neighbour who had called the police pointed to the house where the boys lived.

The policeman knocked on the door of the house and asked the mother if her sons were home. She played dumb and said they were outside playing and she didn't know where they were.

The officer then asked if somebody in the house owned a gun. When she nodded he asked her if she was aware that her children were playing with it and had just shot somebody.

According to Erwin a long and heated discussion followed with the mother saying it must have been an accident and she doesn't know how the children got a hold of the gun because her husband uses it for hunting and normally locks it in a safe place.

After many tears and hand-wringing by the mother proclaiming her poor children to be good kids and that it will never happen again, the cop waving his finger in her face while lecturing her, he turned to Erwin and said; "What do you want from her to reimburse you for your troubles?"

Erwin was stunned, he didn't expect that question but said; "Well, the drugstore, the nurse and the doctor charged me about $45.00 and a new phone card might cost another $5.00, so I guess $50.00 should cover everything."

The officer looked at him and said, "That's all? Nothing for pain and suffering?"

When Erwin said that he just wanted his expenses covered, the cop turned to the mother and asked her if she had $50.00 in the house to cover the damage. She went to the kitchen, got the money and gave it to the officer who turned to Erwin and said,

"That's it now? You are happy with that and everything is settled?"

When Erwin nodded in agreement the cop got into his cruiser and took off after directing a few more words with a warning to the mother to watch her kids and the gun.

I can just imagine what would have happened in a similar situation in Toronto.

Somebody would have called the police and freaked out that a gunman is sitting on a rooftop shooting at people. A SWAT Team would have come in, sealed off the neighbourhood and started searching for the two perpetrators.

After establishing that two juveniles committed the crime Children's Aid would have been called, the boys would have been sent to a youth detention centre and held for questioning and counselling.

The parents would be charged with negligence and unsafe storage of a firearm.

A personal injury law firm with a towering advertising presence on local TV and radio would contact Erwin to advise him that he can sue for pain and suffering as well as mental anguish and psychiatrists would testify that Erwin suffers from recurring nightmares and bouts of depression.

The case against the boys would go to juvenile court and they would be sentenced to six months in a detention facility.

The parents would be convicted of their crimes and get a suspended sentence and have to attend a firearms education program, pay a heavy fine and pay for the court costs.

The civil case would drag on and Erwin would be awarded a million dollars of which the law firm would collect one third for their fee.

The guilty party would lose their house to pay the damages. Now unable to find work, because they are homeless and have a criminal record, their sons would have to quit school to support their parents, turning to a life of crime after realizing that life and our legal system aren't fair.

I think fifty bucks, a stern lecture and a hell of a fright for everybody was just as effective. In addition, a good hiding for the boys when Daddy came home that night was possibly more useful than six months of counselling.

You've got to love Mexican Justice!

✺ Chapter 5

Laughing In Church?

I have never been a very religious person but I always assumed certain things about Christianity.

My belief was that having faith makes Christians happy, joyful and makes it easy to laugh and enjoy life. That believing in a forgiving God and the existence of heaven and an afterlife would be enough to make your existence on this earth enjoyable and allow you to laugh at adversity.

I am also one of these people who does not often go to church except for weddings, funerals and other special occasions where we are told that God and Jesus take care of us.

The only other times Jackie and I visit churches and cathedrals is when we travel and admire the impressive architecture, splendour and works of art Christianity has to offer.

On our last trip we visited many Churches in Germany, Croatia and Spain and when we looked at all the paintings and sculptures inside and outside of these marvellous houses of worship it occurred to me to ask,

Why is there no or very little laughter in Christianity?

Why are there no pictures of a laughing, giggling baby Jesus?

Why are there no pictures of a laughing, joyful Jesus Christ?

Why are there no pictures of a happy and joyful Virgin Mary holding a smiling baby Jesus?

Why are there no paintings of laughing or happy people?

We have never been in a church that exhibits a happy face or a laughing face or a joyful image in paintings or sculptures. A content or consoling image is as far as positive expressions go, but laughter... nowhere to be seen.

That observation prompted me to Google if there are any references in the bible of Jesus actually laughing.

There are none.

How about Googling if there are any references in the whole bible about laughter?

There are only 42 mentions of laughter in the bible. The Bible does say that God laughs. In the Psalms it's a derisive laugh. When the kings of the world set themselves against God and take counsel against God, it says that he who sits in the heavens shall laugh. God will hold them in derision. It's sort of a "huh!" kind of laughter. It's not a jovial response of happiness, but nevertheless it's laughter.

I found an article by Tamal Frankiel that poses an interesting question, and I quote;

"Why have we not been able to laugh at religion? Underneath it all, are we afraid to take religion lightly? That a wrathful deity might put up with all kinds of other crimes against humanity, life and even lack of devotion to Himself, but not with being laughed at?

"Would the creator of humanity, who made the world completely good, regret creating a laughing being more than a murderous one? This would be an ironic theological outcome for Western religions. Not that Buddhism, Confucianism, Taoism or Hinduism are known for rollicking laugh-fests."

So what is it that makes Christians happy and upbeat?

My conclusion is that it is the music.

Again, we don't really find the word laugh or laughter in traditional or religious music but there are uplifting happy pieces like *'Joy to the World'*. Many gospel songs express happiness and jubilation and are a pleasure to listen, even dance or sway to and put smiles on our faces and joy in our hearts.

It is however the more modern secular Christmas season songs that feature laughter and humour in their lyrics, like Jingle Bells, Silver Bells and Rudolph, just to name a few.

So a church is possibly not the best place to look for laughter or joy.

But if you travel and want to be truly awed and impressed by religion inspired architecture and art and want to find a quiet place of contemplation, churches are a good place to visit.

Chapter 6

Fast Food In Peru

The local cuisine in any place always interests me. I make sure to try and sample at least one unique dish in every country we visit. Jackie has, however, refused some of the local delicacies I've tasted. Here is a little selection of things I've tried...

I've eaten crocodile, alligator, rattlesnake, chocolate covered grasshoppers, a scorpion, rotten eggs and bird nests just to name a few.

Some of these were delicious and others I couldn't finish after the first bite. There are, however, dishes that sound absolutely terrible but are not repulsive after you know that the name of the dish has nothing to do with the actual ingredients, like the 'Monkey Gland Burger', a South African delicacy. Monkey-gland sauce is just spicy BBQ sauce without any monkey meat or glands of any kind in it.

When we got to Peru I was surprised to find out that the guinea pig plays an important part in many cultures of indigenous South American groups, especially as a food source. Many restaurants have them on their menu and I was definitely going to try a guinea pig dish.

Jackie remembered the guinea pig we had bought our daughter as a pet. We had named it Cowlick for her unruly tufts of hair growing in all directions. The whole family got quite attached to Cowlick at the time. However, I wondered right away how closely related this adorable looking rodent is to the most repugnant rodent of them all, the rat.

Even though these were two good reasons not to eat a guinea pig I was ready to have this little rodent for lunch one day.

On our trip through the Sacred Valley of the Incas on the way to Machu Picchu we came to the small town of Pisac. There we climbed up the mountain side to explore the archeological sight of Qalla Q'asa, also known as The Citadel. The architecture of the Citadel left me questioning how these relatively small-in-stature people got these massive stones to the top of the mountain to build this magnificent fortress. It was not only the climb to its three thousand meter high elevation that took my breath away but also the view overlooking this fertile valley carved out by the Willkanuta River. The steep sides of the mountains had been terraced by the Incas to enable agriculture and local farmers still work them today, more than fifteen hundred years later.

Sitting on a huge rock that was part of the impressive wall surrounding the fortress I was taking in this unforgettable sight marvelling at man's and nature's ability to cooperate in order to create unforgettable things of beauty.

When we returned to Pisac we were thirsty and hungry and needed a rest. Our tour guide gave us an hour to explore the local market and possibly try one or two of the local delicacies or buy one of the many handmade blankets, purses or rugs.

I noticed an open grill and asked our guide what the cook was offering. "He is grilling guinea pigs," he told me.

"Just what I am looking for," I thought. Jackie declined trying one with me, so I went over to experience the taste of a guinea pig all by myself.

My Spanish is very limited but with the help of sign language the cook understood my request and pointed to a cage full of guinea pigs and made me understand that I should pick the one I wanted and he would slaughter it, skin it and throw it on the grill for me.

Looking at him in disbelief and glancing at the cage with these cute little rodents squealing and whistling as if they knew what was going to happen to them, I shook my head and walked away. I could not bring myself to watch the execution of one of these little critters that I would have sentenced to death and then eat it. They reminded me too much of my daughters little pet Cowlick, with whom we cuddled and played.

Guinea pig remains the only local dish in a foreign country I have refused to eat. Who could eat the family pet?

I wonder how many buckets of chicken KFC would sell if you would have to pick your chicken, watch them kill it, pluck it, then hack it to pieces and fry it.

On the other hand maybe we should start a fast food chain serving chicken, rabbit and guinea pig with the motto: 'Pick Your Own Critter' and call it:

'Kill and Grill'

Bon Appetite!

TRAV-EL-ATIONS

❈ Chapter 7

Riding The Rails In Africa

There is no way of travel more relaxing, enjoyable and romantic than a journey by train.

We have travelled on all kinds of trains from ultra-modern bullet trains to historical tourist trains using old steam locomotives from days gone by. None of them were as memorable as the ones we took in South Africa. They are unforgettable for completely different, almost opposite reasons.

Trip 1: Cape Town To Johannesburg

It was 2001 and we were on our world trip. We originally planned to travel by car from Cape Town to Johannesburg but changed our minds when we heard about the once-a-week run of what was called 'The Poor Man's Blue Train'.

The original Blue Train is one of the most luxurious trains in the world and rivals and even exceeds the fabled Orient Express or the Trans-Siberian Railroad.

A two-day trip on this train, all meals, drinks and excursions included, now starts at about C$ 1,500.00.*

The so called Poor Man's Blue Train was at that time only about

$200.00 per person for the 27-hour trip and included all meals, wine with dinner, a welcome reception and a private sleeper compartment for two with 24-hour butler service.

The choice was clear, a romantic adventure waited for us and we were not disappointed.

When we boarded, the butler carried our luggage to our compartment and told us to get settled in and then come to the dining car for the departure reception.

The selection of hors d'oeuvres was overwhelming and we were offered Mimosas or just plain South African champagne.

Since I love champagne and the waiter kept filling my glass whenever I emptied it, I was quite happy when the train pulled out of the station.

I had a tough time keeping my eyes open due to the alcohol induced sleepiness and the constant clickety-clack of the wheels but the breathtaking scenery and the frequent blowing of the train's whistle kept me awake.

Leaving Cape Town and rolling into the wine region of the Cape province you can't avoid noticing the stark contrast of the ultra rich and the destitute that still exists today. Passing shanty towns where cardboard boxes and corrugated iron shacks without electricity or running water are the homes of blacks and the lavish estates of white farmers in the distance show that the inequality and the fruits of oppression of the Apartheid era are not yet erased.

Approaching the Hex Mountains the train enters a series of tunnels, the longest being over 13 kilometres long. When we came out of the tunnels the countryside had changed dramatically.

(*All dollar values given in this story are in Canadian currency based on the exchange rate at the time.)

We were now in the Little Karoo, a semi dessert. This area has an abundance of wildlife but don't expect to see elephants, lions or giraffes. We saw lots of baboons, various breeds of sheep, mountain goats and birds of prey not being bothered by the train rumbling past.

It was now getting dark and the butler asked us to proceed to the dining car.

The four-course dinner was spectacular and accompanied by the best South African wine.

When we returned to our compartment the staff had transformed our seating area into a comfortable sleeping arrangement.

This time the clickety-clack and the wine induced drowsiness made us fall asleep almost immediately - although we woke up a few times during the night due to the frequent stops along the route and the sound of the train whistle every time we pulled into a station.

The breakfast was delicious and when we returned to our compartment it had been restored to a comfortable sitting room.

The train now stopped mainly in African townships and children were selling all kinds of local fruits to passengers looking out of their open windows.

As the train got going again I saw something flying by me and then a grape hit me.

Some boys would bombard the unsuspecting passengers with unsold fruit. We found at least a dozen grapes, apples and apricots in our compartment.

At the next stop we knew to close our widow quickly when the conductor blew his whistle. I guess boys will be boys and up to no good in any part of the world.

We were now approaching Johannesburg passing the gold fields and gold mines that where probably the ugliest part of the countryside we saw on this unforgettable trip.

Johannesburg station was bustling with people and we were happy to see Jackie's nephew waiting for us on the platform as we arrived.

Trip 2: Cape Town to Stellenbosch

In 2013 we returned to Cape Town and, fondly remembering our fantastic train trip to Johannesburg, we decided to hit the rails again. This time we booked a wine tasting tour in Stellenbosch. We had to get to Stellenbosch by train where a driver would pick us up to visit seven wineries.

We were in a cozy B&B in one of the more picturesque parts of Cape Town known as the Bo-Kaap or the Malay Quarters as it was called during Apartheid days. We were a ten-minute walk away from the central train station and the day before our little excursion we took a walk to the station to purchase our return tickets.

The man at the ticket booth asked if we wanted coach tickets or if we preferred the 'Plus' fare. The tickets were only around $4.00 per person return and I asked him how much the regular ticket would be.

"Only $2.40," he replied. "Would you prefer the regular fare sir?"

" Oh no," I said." It's so cheap and too tempting to pass up for an hour-and-twenty minute ride in first class."

The next morning we showed up early to board and get a good seat. We found our train but all the cars looked the same. We walked up and down to see where first class was or at least a marking for 'Plus Class' as our ticket read.

We asked a young lady if she could tell us which cars are designated as Plus Class and she informed us that it is always the last three cars of the train to Stellenbosch and the same on the way back. We thanked her and went to the back to board.

We didn't think we were in the right place when we entered the compartment.

The walls were full of graffiti, the windows were all scratched up and the seats were torn and repaired with duct-tape. Even though the floors had been swept, the whole car needed a good scrub down, a paint job and some extensive upholstery work.

Not a pretty sight.

We were just about to get off the train, because we surely must have gotten the wrong advice, when the young lady we talked to earlier boarded as well. We asked her if she was sure this was Plus Class and she confirmed her earlier advice to us.

"If this is 1st class what does economy look like and what is the difference?" I asked.

Her answer surprised me.

"The cars are all the same," she said. "The only difference is that the front part of the train only has one armed guard but every car in Plus Class has its own guard and tickets are never oversold so you are assured of a seat. These are the only differences."

"However," she continued,"if you want to have peace and quiet you travel Plus Class since the poor Africans can hardly afford the regular price to commute to and from work."

Hmm, I thought, it's now economic Apartheid to keep the Blacks separate.

The young lady kept talking and told us that it is much more fun to ride in economy. The Africans sing their tribal songs and invite everybody to join in, clapping and swaying to the beat. Preachers make the rounds to preach fire and brimstone and praise the Lord. Some people bring chickens and other small domestic animals on board that contribute to the noise with their barking, clucking or hissing.

"It's a hoot,"she said. "You should try it on your way back."

The 90-minute ride on our part of the train was quiet and uneventful.

Our guide was waiting for us as we arrived in Stellenbosch.

The wine tour was extremely enjoyable with one exception.

Almost every estate had a shanty town attached outside their boundaries where the black labourers lived, often without the most basic amenities. At the same time, most estate owners had a fleet of luxury cars parked in their multi-garage mansions but still had the audacity to complain about not being able to afford to pay their workers a living wage or supply decent housing for their seasonal employees. At that time the South African labour unions were fighting to increase the basic minimum wage of about $5.00 per day. Many countries at that time had a fair wage policy and would not import wines from wineries that did not offer a living wage. Canada was one of them.

We certainly tried many different wines, red, white and sparkling as well as fortified wines and some brandies.

Every winery supplied you with a spittoon and you were supposed to simply taste the wine and refrain from swallowing. We definitely considered that a waste of excellent samples and insisted on enjoying every sip to its logical conclusion and kept the spittoon empty.

After the fifth winery we asked our guide to take us back to the train station to catch an earlier train.

We were bombed!

We considered joining the Africans in economy but quickly realized we weren't in any state to enjoy the noise and revelry. Instead we enjoyed a nice little nap all the way back to Cape Town.

I guess we were still drunk when we arrived and the walk back to our B&B was suddenly too much of a challenge.

We hailed a cab.

South Africa's tourist ads boast that they are 'A World In One Country' and that is certainly true when it comes to travelling by train. They cater to the richest and the poorest and show you a world of luxury and extreme poverty along the way.

Truly, a world of both extremes in one country.

The Beginning

✺ Chapter 8

In Mexico 5x6 Equals 40

Bargaining is a way of life in Mexico. You are expected to bargain with the street vendors, souvenir sellers at the beach and also at their many open-air markets.

However, pricing in traditional stores and restaurants are normally set and non-negotiable.

We have heard many creative approaches to get tourists to buy trinkets, with phrases like "It's so cheap it's almost free" to "You tell me how much you want to pay".

One street vendor approached me and I told him I wasn't interested in his wares. He just looked at me and said: "But señor, they are free today."

I fell for it and answered, "OK, let me see what you've got."

He shot right back, "So you are interested, we just have to agree on the price."

Clever line, I laughed but did not buy anything from him.

Most vendors in Mexico have a good sense of humour and don't pester you if you give them a firm but friendly "No thank you."

Sometimes you run into situations where pricing is outrageous and the seller is unreasonably stubborn like in the following instance.

Jackie and I had gone on a little excursion to the colonial city of

IT'S JUST ME!

Campeche from our winter home in the Yucatan. We were joined by a couple of friends all of us stayed in the Hotel Castlemar in the historic part of town.

The one drawback to the hotel was that it did not have a bar.

When we returned from sightseeing and a great dinner in one of the many excellent restaurants in Campeche we still felt like having a drink with our friends but had no beer or wine in our room.

I asked the clerk at the front desk where I could buy a bottle of wine and he told me that there were no liquor stores or supermarkets close by.

The restaurant across the street where we had lunch earlier in the day was still open and I went across the street to ask the owner if he would sell me a bottle of wine. He said all his wines are the same price, 400 pesos per bottle. It seemed rather expensive to pay the equivalent of forty Canadian dollars for a bottle of wine that sells for no more than $10 dollars in the store.

I also remembered that we paid 60 pesos for a glass of wine at lunch, so I asked the owner how many glasses he gets out of a bottle.

" I get about five glasses out of a bottle," he replied

" Well," I said, "if you charge 60 pesos per glass, that would come to $300 Pesos for the bottle."

"Yes," he answered, "but I charge 400 pesos for the bottle."

" I tell you what," I countered," why don't you pour me five glasses of wine and then give me the empty bottle?"

"No señor," he answered," It's 400 pesos if you want the bottle."

"That's ridiculous," I told him, "you don't have to pour the wine, don't have to serve them at the table and have no glasses to wash.""

"That's not ridiculous, that's the price for a bottle of wine," he proclaimed.

There was no amount of reasoning to change his mind. He would rather not give in to my very logical arguments and forgo a sale than be defeated by a Gringo who was telling him how to set his prices.

We still had a good evening in our room drinking Coke and Perrier from the little corner store next to our hotel.

I had a similar incident happen at our local farmer's market in Brampton.

Last summer I spotted a local farmer selling his corn and his sign read;

      Fresh Corn On The Cob
      $5.00 A Dozen
      Or
      40¢ Each

Somehow the math looked wrong and I told the Farmer that 12 cobs at ¢40 only comes to $4.80.

"I know," he said, "but you are the first one who noticed and I've sold many dozens at $5.00"

"What do you do if somebody calls you out on it?" I asked

"I give him two extra cobs at no charge," he answered.

I just wanted six cobs and he said he'd give me seven for $2.50.

"Deal!" I said and both of us were happy.

The Mexican probably would have offered me seven for $3.00, by saying, "I'll make you a deal you can't refuse!"

•••••

Epilogue;

Two years later we went back to the same hotel. This time we made sure to stock up on beverages for our evening cocktails. Just for fun I went across the street and asked again for the price of a bottle of wine. The prices on his menu had not changed and I don't know if he remembered me but with a grin on his face he looked me straight in the eye and said:

"400 Pesos!"

✼ Chapter 9

Samba In The Streets Of Rio

It was February in Rio and one could feel that Carnival was almost upon us. We visited the Sambodromo, the parade street where the annual Carnival parades take place. We watched several dancing groups practising in their costumes to perfect their routines and getting into the mood for the big event. We could only imagine the screaming crowds encouraging the dancers to sway, contort and shake their bodies to the intoxicating beat of the Samba.

Unfortunately, we would leave Rio before the actual parades in March.

On our last night in Rio we decided to book a Samba show at a nightclub to experience the excitement of the Samba music with its mesmerizing and exhilarating beat and the sexy male and female dancers in their fabulous, revealing costumes driving the audience into a frenzy.

We were not disappointed.

The show finished around midnight and we got onto our tour bus to take us and other tourists back to our respective hotels.

Most of the hotels were along Atlantic Boulevard that runs along Ipanema and Copacabana Beaches. Our hotel, the Intercontinental, was at the end of Copacabana Beach and we were the last ones to be dropped off. A few blocks away from the hotel I noticed a policeman in the middle of the street waving a flashlight, forcing the bus driver to turn off Atlantic Boulevard to take a detour along a parallel street and rejoin the Boulevard a block later.

I leaned forward to ask the driver what the reason for the detour was since it was past midnight on a Sunday and there would surely be no construction going on at this time of night..

His answer perplexed me.

"Didn't you see the group of party people dancing and drumming away in the middle of the road? There must have been at least 40 or 50 of them," he said.

"You let them dance in the middle of the road and obstruct traffic? And the police lets them get away with it?" I enquired.

"Look", he said, " it would take at least ten policemen in four cruisers to disperse the crowd and make sure they don't start again further down the road. It only takes two officers to let them have their fun and reroute the few cars that are on Atlantic Boulevard after midnight ."

I wondered how many cop-cars would show up in Toronto if 40 kids started dancing on Yonge Street at midnight on a Sunday.

"Hmm," I thought, "maybe we should hire Brazilian Police officers for riot prevention at home."

✲ Chapter 10

Adventures Of A *Schlachtenbummler*

Schlachtenbummler is another one of those German words that has no equal in English. It is a compound word comprised of Schlacht, meaning battle, and bummler, meaning loafer or stroller.

It describes a sports fan who follows his team to away games, or a travelling fan who seeks good sporting competitions.

A globetrotting sports fan.

The Soccer World Cup, or Football as it is called everywhere but North America, is held every four years in a different part of the World.

I have travelled twice to become a Schlachtenbummler, in both 1974 and 2006 when the World Cup was held in Germany.

The atmosphere, the enthusiasm of the people attending the games, the fans from all the different countries of the world, the genuine love of the sport and the truly friendly spirit of all the people is something you don't get by watching the games in front of the TV.

World Cup 1974

In 1974 I travelled with two South African friends, Colin and Terry Lesch, who just wanted to be part of this greatest single sport competition in the world. I of course was a fan of the German National Team but we travelled all around Germany and attended many games of different nations. Experiencing the enthusiasm and devotion of fans from other countries and their way to support, cheer on and celebrate their team's victories or suffer with their players in defeat was incredible.

It was actually a gruelling schedule we had laid out but we were young and didn't mind the travelling, the late nights celebrating with other soccer fans and a diet consisting of street food and overpriced stadium fast food. In Germany that mainly consisted of sausages of all kinds and beer.

We had bought all our tickets in Canada through a licenced travel agency that was given a block of tickets by FIFA, the international football association. There was no chance of getting additional tickets in Germany since the games had sold out quickly in this soccer crazy nation

We flew from Toronto direct to Frankfurt and arrived early in the morning to grey skies, rain and all-around miserable weather. We picked up our rental car and drove straight to the stadium to attend the opening ceremonies and the opening game, traditionally the defending champion against their first-round opponent. In this case it was Brazil playing against Yugoslavia.

We only had standing room tickets. In those days stadia were not required to offer seats for every fan. We waited for five hours in a steady rain interrupted by periods of drizzle and stretches of cold mist for the festivities to begin. This after having sat in an airplane for eight hours and missing a night of sleep.

Thankfully the ceremonies were truly fantastic. All 16 nations were represented and had arrived in giant collapsing soccer balls. Each country's representatives were dressed in their national costumes and the performance of the Samba Band and dance troupe cheered us up and made us forget that we were dead tired and soaking wet. Mercifully the speeches were short and it was great to see all the famous soccer players of the past in person as they were introduced, from Germany's Uwe Seeler to Brazil's Pele.

The game between Brazil and Yugoslavia finally started at 5:00 pm and was less than thrilling.

Even though there were glimpses of brilliance, neither team wanted to lose and played to a boring 0-0 tie.

The game finished at about 7:00 pm. We had been in the stadium in miserable weather for ten hours and had to drive to Berlin where my mother waited to welcome us. We arrived shortly after 1 am.

After a late snack, my mother insisted we had to have, Colin and Terry went to bed. I still spent an hour talking to my mother who hadn't seen me for more than a year.

We slept in the next morning. However we had to leave that afternoon to make it to Berlin's historic Olympic stadium to watch Germany's opening game against Chile. It was another fairly uneventful game but I was delighted, Germany won 1-0.

We spent the next three days in Berlin. I introduced Terry and Colin to my old friends who welcomed them with open arms. Sightseeing during the day, pub-hopping in the evenings and a luncheon with my cousins filled the time we had. Colin and Terry became quickly enamoured with Berlin's pubs. My mother spoiled us as much as she could and possibly enjoyed spoiling us even more than we enjoyed being spoiled.

After three days of rest it was off to Dortmund to watch the Netherlands play Sweden. It was an entertaining game but still ended in a scoreless draw. We stayed two nights in Dortmund before travelling to Hamburg to watch the highly anticipated first ever match between West Germany and East Germany.

Hamburg was our most adventurous stop for more than one reason. This was before the Internet days and to make reservations for a room you relied on travel agents, yellow pages, personal recommendations, newspaper ads and the local tourist information kiosk found in every city. There was no Travelocity or TripAdvisor to read up on customer ratings and reviews. I don't remember how we booked it but we ended up in the most dreadful pension in Hamburg.

Pensions are what Germans call guesthouses or B&Bs. It was a scary looking mansion where every room appeared to have been rented to mean or half-dead comatose elderly men. The incredible stench wafting through the dimly lit house was suggestive of many unwashed pets being boarded along with their owners.

I guess that's what you sometimes run into when you are travelling on a budget.

Breakfast was included and was quite delicious. The smell of omelettes, excellent coffee and freshly baked bread filled the dining room. By morning our nostrils had become acclimatized to the odour and the nauseous feeling we had when we entered the 'House of Foul Aromas' was gone.

We left for the Volksparkstadion to witness the historic game of West Germany versus East Germany.

As we reached the entrance, passing armed policemen and lots of security guards along the way, I reached into my back pocket to present my ticket at the gate.

It was gone! I had been pick-pocketed.

I panicked!

We went to a policeman to report my stolen ticket. He lead us to the public relations tent and a FIFA official and local police listened to my story. We told them that we were a bunch of Canadians all sitting in the same section and they could see that the ticket between Terry's and Colin's seats was the one I had.

They believed our story and escorted me to my seat. They also placed a plain-clothes policeman at the aisle to catch the thief when he arrived to take my place.

He showed up 10 minutes before kick-off.

When questioned he admitted to having bought the ticket outside the stadium for an exorbitant price. He had tears in his eyes while he pleaded with the policeman not to arrest him or kick him out. By this point we were feeling pretty bad for this poor guy and we joined in to plead with the officer to let him stay.

Our seats were on a long bench with seat numbers painted on it and we offered to squeeze together to make room for him.

Common sense prevailed. The officer agreed that no harm was done and if we were happy with him staying he would be okay with it too.

The game was about to begin.

Let me start by painting a bit of a background to this monumental event in German sports history.

West Germany had already qualified for the next round and so had East Germany. It was just a question who would win the group and who would place second. The truth was that both sides wanted to win badly, the West Germans to avoid embarrassment, the East Germans to prove they belonged on the same international football stage as their countrymen from the other side of the iron curtain.

In a boring game where nobody wanted to do much for fear of losing it was looking like another scoreless tie when East Germany scored the winning goal with eight minutes left to play.

I left the stadium not knowing whether I should cry for losing to the East Germans or be delighted knowing we would not have to face either Brazil, Argentina or the Netherlands until the final.

East Germany, who ended up winning the group, now paradoxically faced the tougher challenges of Brazil, Argentina and the Netherlands in the next round, and was eliminated. West Germany on the other hand, had an easier draw with Poland, Sweden and Yugoslavia. They ended up winning the rest of their matches, including the final against the Netherlands, becoming world champions, erasing the humiliation of losing to East Germany.

Our final adventure was a visit to Hamburg's 'Red Light District', a street called the Reeperbahn.

Here you could be a voyeur or a participant in any kind of sex show you can imagine, or rent one of the scantily dressed ladies of the evening for an hour. There were many of them, of all shapes and colours, sitting in store windows showing off their wares, waiting for a customer to come and have their way with them.

Terry and Colin, having come from puritanical Canada and grown up in not only sexually oppressed South Africa, had never seen anything like it. Judging by their reactions to this Sodom and Gomorrah environment, They were shocked, but not necessarily in a negative or repulsive way.

I can assure my readers that we, clean cut young men, simply went there to study the depraved sexual behaviour of other people and only watched and never touched.

After another night in our stinky castle we departed for Munich, an 800-kilometre drive.

We got to Munich in less than eight hours. Colin was not happy with the lack of speed limits on the Autobahn and reminded me he was a father-to-be and wanted to get home in one piece to hold his baby-to- be in his arms. Terry didn't object to me driving at close to 200km/

hr and enjoyed the rush that speed will give you.

We checked into a much more pleasant, non-smelly pension when we arrived and spent the rest of the evening enjoying a Bavarian beer garden and a dose of real um-pa-pa music.

The next morning we explored a bit more of the city and drove to the Munich Olympic stadium to watch Haiti against Argentina.

The game didn't mean anything for either team. Argentina had already won the group and Haiti was eliminated from further competition. It ended up being the most entertaining game we had witnessed so far.

Argentina won easily 4:1 but I'll never forget the jubilation when the Haitians scored against the former world champions. The stadium erupted to a standing ovation celebrating the achievements of the underdog. Haiti went home not winning a single game and scoring only two goals, but they both came against powerhouses of international soccer, Italy and Argentina.

That was victory in its own right.

We drove back to Berlin after the game to spend the rest of our time there. We had no more tickets and there were no more matches scheduled in Berlin.

Terry had to go home the following week since he only had two weeks of vacation. Colin and I watched the rest of the games with my friends, in pubs or at my mother's house.

We had a ball. Colin became very popular among my friends and our last evening in my old pub, which was essentially my second home before I immigrated, was unbelievable. The innkeeper, 'Red Inge' as she was called for her Rita Hayworth-like flowing red hair, gave Colin a send-off which he might never forget. We partied until long after four o'clock in the morning with Inge not keeping a tab but everyone paying what they felt they owed.

The sun was coming up as we waddled home, feeling no pain.

The next day was the final of the World Cup. We had decided to watch it with my friend Kalle at his place.

When I tried to wake Colin up at about 2:00 pm to go to Kalle's apartment. I could not get him up. He was practically unconscious. By 2.30 pm he successfully managed to get up but on his way to the bathroom he missed the door and walked straight into the wall. We assisted him to get his business done but no amount of cold water in his face nor the delicious smell or taste of my mother's hot coffee would resuscitate him. He went back to bed.

We debated calling a doctor as we thought that he might have a mild case of alcohol poisoning but ultimately decided against it.

With just minutes to go before the game we managed to drag him in front of the TV, propping him up in a big armchair. Wrapped in a blanket he was a sad sight to look at.

By the time the game ended he had recovered enough to join us for a stroll down the Kurfürstendamm, Berlin's main boulevard, to celebrate Germany's win. It was a terrific street party with no violence or hooliganism. However all of us were feeling the aftermath of the previous night and we left the festivities early.

I do not think Colin saw much of the final game between Germany and the Netherlands because when we got home he enjoyed the rerun of the game shown on TV that night and reacted to every goal like he had never seen it before.

We left for Canada the next morning having had the time of our lives as Schlachtenbummler.

World Cup 2006

What a difference 32 years make.

The experience of 2006 was totally different from 1974.

In many ways it was better but there were many disappointments as well. Almost all of it was driven by advancement in technology.

Neither my friend Kalle nor I were able to get any tickets we desired, except on the black market at horrendous prices. Tickets were sold through a worldwide lottery which both of us entered and ended up with tickets for games of lesser nations, no Germany, Spain, Italy, Brazil or Argentina.

In 1974 we just booked our flights with a German travel agency in Toronto and got as many tickets as we wanted. In 2006 I had to buy a package with pre-selected games, flights, hotel accommodation and transportation between stadia at highly inflated prices and no extra tickets for people who would want to join me in Germany.

So Kalle and I bought the tickets offered in the lottery.

I arrived on the 5th of June in Berlin and three days later we were off to Bochum.

We had chosen Bochum as our four-day home because it is located in the middle of Dortmund and Gelsenkirchen where our first game, Poland against Ecuador, took place.

We had two stadia within a 30-minute drive of our B&B and Cologne was less than an hour's drive away. It was the perfect location to possibly scalp some extra tickets and the 30,000 seat stadium in Bochum showed every game on their giant screens on each end of the field. The daily entrance fee was only five Euros and the beer and food were cheap and delicious.

What else could a *Schlachtenbummler* want?

We spent a couple of afternoons and evenings on the infield watching games with fans from all over the world. It was always a festive atmosphere with fans dressed up in their national outfits or colours showing with which teams their allegiances were lying. Some fans showed up in the most ridiculous and humorous outfits which contributed to the fun and frivolity.

We were also lucky to get a pair of tickets from a scalper for the Czech Republic against USA game. It cost us a small fortune but was still within our budget and affordable.

What a delight this game was. Most of the American fans were so confident, almost arrogantly positive that their team, ranked much higher than the little Czech Republic, would absolutely annihilate their opponents.

It didn't quite work out that way. The US was soundly beaten by a score of 3-0 to the delight of the mostly pro-Czech crowd.

After that game Kalle and I decided to go back to Berlin since we didn't have any tickets for the next few days.

The atmosphere in Berlin was breathtaking and electric for every game. FIFA and the German organizers had built what was called 'The Fan Mile', a strip of giant screens on a mil-long boulevard stretching from the famous Brandenburg Gate to Berlin's other prominent monument,'The Victory Column' with souvenir stands and beer gardens every few meters along the way.

It was a party every day.

Here is how Deutsche Welle, a German broadcaster described the fan mile:

With its World Cup fan mile, Berlin gave Munich's Oktoberfest a run for its money in the stakes as the ultimate party draw -- and won, say officials from the German Tourism Office.

In a little north-south rivalry, Berlin topped Munich with its fan mile.

It was a cliche-buster, that's for sure. With nary a dirndl or pair of lederhosen in sight, with soccer -- not beer -- as the main attraction, Berlin's fan mile managed to outstrip the Munich Oktoberfest and claim the title of party of the year. According to the German Tourism Office, nine million people flocked to the Berlin boulevard where giant screens broadcast the World Cup matches. In contrast, the annual Oktoberfest in the southern city of Munich only manages to attract a paltry six million visitors.

The atmosphere at the fan mile was so friendly and peace-loving that a little old lady could have ventured into the crowds with her handbag dangling loosely and not have been robbed.

I have to wholeheartedly agree with this description. Neither Kalle nor I ever had so much fun at a street party. I might add that Kalle initially did not want to go because he hated crowds, but ended up turning every stranger he me into a new friend.

The spirit, the atmosphere, the friendliness and lack of hostility towards other fans was incredible. All this in spite of the fact that the beer was flowing freely. In fact the beer was one of the biggest contributing factors to the celebratory mood.

After enjoying Berlin's fan mile we had one more trip, a game in Leipzig, It was just a day trip about 200 kilometres away. The game was Angola against Iran. Neither one of us was looking forward to driving three hours to watch a game where both teams had already been eliminated from further competition.

We could not have been more wrong.

We expected some booing towards the Iranians but none was forthcoming. It was again a friendly and festive atmosphere. The crowd was heavily pro-Angola and we were happy to be right in the middle of a group of Angolans dressed in their national tribal outfits, primarily red and black, armed with drums and in a party mood to celebrate and enjoy the last game their national team would play in this competition. It was an entertaining contest with the Iranians also playing an open style of soccer to please not only their supporters but everybody in the stands.

We drove back home the same evening and got ready for our last game to which we had tickets. It was in Berlin's fabled Olympic Stadium where 80,000 spectators came to watch a deciding game that would determine who would continue and who would go home.

Ukraine against Tunisia.

With a win either team would advance, but a tie would send Tunisia home. We expected an exciting game, but it turned out to be disappointingly boring. The most entertaining bit was watching the Tunisians dance and party in the large entrance plaza of the stadium. The Ukrainian spectators did not put on much of a show even though they outnumbered the Tunisians by a lot.

The same was true during the game. Tunisia was reduced to ten men in the second half due to a red card for one of their players but was the better team in the second half.

It took a penalty shot in the 70th minute for Ukraine to score in this poorly refereed game.

The game ended without us. We were so bored that we left a few minutes early to avoid the rush out of the stadium.

The preliminary round was over, we had no more tickets for the remainder of the tournament and getting any on the black market was prohibitively expensive and out of reach.

However the Berlin Senate in cooperation with Adidas did something never before done at any World Cup, possibly because the technology did not exist before.

During the World Cup, a temporary stadium was to be build in front of the Reichstag, home to Germany's parliament, providing a place in the heart of Berlin where fans could watch public screenings of the games.

The stadium was a replica of Berlin's Olympic Stadium on a scale of 1:3.3. Up to 10,000 fans could sit in the arena which cost Adidas tens of millions of Euros to build. All 64 World Cup games were broadcast on giant screens on the grounds at the Reichstag. Adidas expected up to 70,000 visitors per day.

Yet the action was not limited to passive spectating.

Around the stadium, soccer fields were set up. Mini tournaments were held. Schools were encouraged to take field trips to the park and play soccer. Also, no World Cup in Germany would be complete without a beer garden. The public in general should have a good time. Even on those few days when soccer players and fans had the day off from the tournament, the mini-stadium hosted concerts. Besides many German musicians international groups like The Black Eyed Peas and artists like English singer-songwriter James Blunt performed on those days.

Watching a game there was the next best thing to being at the Stadium. Kalle had gotten tickets for the quarterfinal Germany - Argentina. We made a day of it and took in all the pregame entertainment and it almost felt like being in the Olympic Stadium just a few miles away.

We had a blast!

I could describe this game for the next ten pages but let's just say it was the longest match I've ever seen. There were boring stretches, yellow cards, amazing goals, fights involving players, fans and referees, overtime and finally a penalty shoot-out with Germany being victorious.

We watched the semi-final, Germany - Italy, in Kalle's home with some of his friends and were heartbroken when Germany lost in the final two minutes of overtime. We drowned our sorrows by emptying Kalle's house bar but had to admit that Italy probably deserved to win. They were the better team that day.

We got seats for the final in Kalle's local soccer club's clubhouse.

The hall, which was also a restaurant, was packed. It was a pleasure to sit and watch the final with players, coaches and referees who loved the game and were passionate, vocal, emotional and most supportive of the French team. However, there were quite a few Italians present who were guest workers and had dressed in their 'Azzuri' team colours and proudly waved their flags.

Again the game went into overtime and had to be decided by penalty shots with Italy being crowned the new World Champion.

After a day of rest and recovery I flew back home, being a happy Schlachtenbummler who didn't see his team win but was happy to be part of the most spectacular single sporting event in the world.

Many people asked me before I left and after I got back if it was worth the money to watch something live that I could have watched for free on TV at home.

Guess what my answer was.

❊ Chapter 11

What Americans believe...

Everybody knows that most Americans don't share the following beliefs, however, after travelling extensively through the US, eating in restaurants and listening mostly to talk radio and religious stations while crossing their beautiful country and following their election rhetoric my observations are that one could easily come to the conclusion that all Americans share the following beliefs:

• Americans believe that the USA is the greatest country in the world.

• Americans believe that you can't have peace without having a war first.

• Americans believe that they have more freedoms than any other people in the world.

• Americans believe in separation of State and Church but America should be run by Christian politicians with Christian beliefs and Christian values.

• Americans believe that Patriotism and Nationalism are the same thing.

• Americans believe that you can't be a racist if you have a friend who is not white.

• Americans believe that the metric system is more complicated

than gallons, miles, yards, feet, inches, ounces, pounds and Fahrenheit.
- Americans believe that their justice system is perfect.
- Americans believe that paying less taxes will reduce the National Debt.
- Americans believe that 'Obama Care' takes away their right to die uninsured.
- Americans believe that all liberals, Canadians and Europeans are closet Communists.
- Americans believe that all Muslims are Terrorists.
- Americans believe that science is wrong if it is not supported by the Scripture.
- Americans believe that soccer is more boring than baseball.
- Americans believe that compromising is a sign of weakness.
- Americans believe that owning guns and enforcing the death penalty make their lives safer.
- Americans believe that the light brown beverage being served to them in most of their restaurants is actually coffee.
- Americans believe that fat, sugar and carbohydrates are the most important food groups.
- Americans believe that there are two kinds of people in the world, Americans and those that want to be Americans.
- Americans believe that hate and fear are good motivators.
- Americans believe that you should love thy neighbours as long as they are white Christians.
- Americans believe that the rich have to get richer so they can work on eliminating poverty in America.
- Americans believe they are well educated and understand the world.
- Americans believe that facts distort the truth.
- Americans believe that God is American and that Jesus wasn't a Jew.

God Bless America

✸ Chapter 12

Smoking And Drinking In Berlin

Germans, like most Europeans, have always been heavy smokers. It took politicians, doctors and non-smokers a long time to convince the public that smoking is a health hazard and that it is pretty annoying for non-smokers to live with second-hand smoke wherever they go.

Until 2008 it was up to restaurant and pub owners to provide non-smoking sections but they were not required to do so. I once asked a waiter for a non-smoking table and he took the ashtray off the table and said, "This is your non-smoking table now."

In 2011 we went to Germany to experience the magic of the Christmas markets one more time. It was the first time that we had to deal with the new non-smoking laws in Berlin. Jackie and I had quit smoking four years earlier and finding non-smoking restaurants was no longer a problem because all restaurants had been designated as such.

Bars and pubs were a different story.

We had walked for three hours through one of Berlin's idyllic Christmas markets on a cold and overcast day looking at arts and crafts and many baked and meat products offered for sale. There were carollers dressed in period costumes walking through the aisles singing traditional German Christmas songs to put everybody in the spirit of the season. The aroma of the glow-wine, the scent of the freshly baked goods, like gingerbread cookies and cinnamon buns, filled the air and the mouth-watering smell of grilled sausages created an uncontrollable craving and built up a healthy appetite.

It was pretty cold and it started to snow when we spotted the old village pub that offered glow-wine, grilled sausages, hamburgers and pretzels on their patio to the patrons of the Christmas market. We decided to go inside the old pub and ordered two glow-wines to warm up while we decided what to eat. We saw our waitress go outside to get our hot drinks from the booth on their patio and when she returned we each ordered a sausage on a bun and a pretzel.

"I'm sorry sir," she said," but you can't eat in here. We are a smoking establishment and we don't serve food."

"But you are serving food outside," I replied," why can't you bring us a couple of sausages? I could even go and get them myself."

"Sir," she said, " if you want to eat you will have to sit outside. This is a smoking pub and no food can be consumed or served where smoking is allowed. That's the law!"

There was no way to explain to her that it is ridiculous for us to have to go outside to eat in the snow in -4°C temperatures while it is perfectly legal to stay inside drink a beer and have a cigarette in the cozy surroundings of a century old pub.

Jackie and I laughed trying to imagine Canadians having to stand outside in the cold to eat a hotdog because they don't have the right to eat while others smoke.

I guess it's the German idea of equal rights for smokers.

If smoking is prohibited where you eat, then eating should be prohibited where smoking is allowed.

Absurd!

✾ Chapter 13

Smoking And Drinking In Cairo

It was our last day in Egypt after ten days of being transported back to Biblical times, the days of pyramids, pharaohs and ancient temples.

After cruising down the Nile from Aswan we were back in Cairo where our visit to this ancient land began ten days earlier.

We were astonished how little had changed in Egypt's countryside since Moses led his people to the Promised Land.

We hardly saw motorized vehicles, just camels and donkeys assisting the farmers in the fields. The nights were black, no neon signs, no street lighting and most houses were illuminated with no more than a 40 Watt bulb.

What struck us most was the sheer size of the temples, pyramids, statues and the relatively great condition they were in; some of them over 4000 years old.

People in the villages wore exclusively traditional Arab and Egyptian clothing. Only tourists and tour guides could be found wearing jeans or T-shirts.

Cairo's downtown however is a modern, bustling city with Western style architecture, supermarkets and fast food chains like McDonald's and KFC. At night bright neon signs illuminate the shores of the Nile and make for a lively atmosphere with elegant restaurants and entertainment. Cairo has the craziest traffic chaos I have ever seen caused mostly by people making up their own rules of the road, or so it appears.

Jackie and I decided to get a taxi and go to the ancient souk of Khan el-Khalili in the centre of the old town. Souks are also called bazaars or casbahs in other parts of the Arab world. We wanted to buy a few souvenirs and experience the excitement and intrigue of an Arabian market place.

Well, we were not disappointed but must say that a souk is certainly not a place for the faint of heart.

Khan el-Khalili is fascinating. The buildings go back as far as 970 AD and the massive gates give the impression that you are entering a medieval fortress. You walk along twisting alleyways and cramped pathways that are so narrow to prevent the sunshine from ever throwing a shadow on the cobblestone pavement. It gives you a feeling of being lost in a labyrinth, impossible to ever find your way out again.

The collection of stores carrying handicrafts, carpets, linen, jewelry, leather goods, sweets and baked goods is breathtaking. The selection of coffee houses and exotic foods, served as street-food or in lovely restaurants, is overwhelming.

We looked into a couple of 'Hookah Lounges' appointed in beautiful oriental decor, where a few men, dressed in smoking jackets and wearing a fez, were sitting on giant pillows smoking hookahs. I would have liked to try it but these lounges are strictly for men and I was not going to let Jackie walk around by herself as I would have never been able to find her again.

It was easy to imagine that we had been transplanted into a movie like 'Casablanca' or 'The Man Who Knew Too Much' and I expected to run into Humphrey Bogart, Jimmy Stewart or Doris Day at any moment.

After two hours of shopping and bargaining I needed a drink and that is often a problem in the Islamic world.

Leaving Khan el-Khalili through its massive gates we entered the large square in front of the impressive Al-Hussain Mosque. There were lots of sidewalk cafes and restaurants and one of the owners approached me to offer us a table.

"I'm sorry," I said," we need a beer, maybe next time."

I was astounded when he said, "Sir, we serve beer in our establishment."

I wanted to get back to our hotel that was serving alcohol in their lounge for their western clientele but was pleased to have found a place to quench my thirst right there in the gorgeous setting of the picturesque centre of town.

I was still smoking in those days and noticed that I was down to my last cigarette and asked if he sold cigarettes.

"I don't," he replied, "but no problem, I'll send one of the street children to buy you a packet."

I saw him walk over to one of the many street urchins lurking around the square to send him off to buy cigarettes.

"Hmm," I thought, "I'm glad to see that I could help one of the kids to make a few pennies."

The little boy came back before our beers were served and the owner brought the beers and the cigarettes at the same time.

The beer bottles were nice and cold but when I took my first sip I almost spit it out.

I looked at the label and read that it was alcohol-free beer. It tasted more like camel-piss than beer.

I called the owner over and complained about not being informed that this was not real beer.

"But," he said, "I thought you knew that it is illegal to consume alcohol within 100 meters of a mosque and we are across the street from the Al-Hussain Mosque, one of our holiest places of worship. I am really sorry for our little misunderstanding but you cannot blame me for your ignorance of Islamic law."

Clever answer, I thought, and just asked for the bill.

At this point I might point out that the lounge in our hotel charges about one dollar for an imported beer and fifty cents for a packet of cigarettes. I expected to pay no more than $2.50 for this horrible beverage and my packet of cigarettes.

"That will be five dollars please," he said while looking at me with a sheepish grin.

"What?" I shouted. "I don't pay more than fifty cents for cigarettes anywhere. How do you come up with five dollars?"

"Oh no!" he cried out, " I have been cheated by a little street-kid. He said the cigarettes were three dollars. How do I know the price, I don't smoke. Oh sir, you can't blame me for my ignorance and make me take a loss. I am distraught about this unfortunate incident."

It was a great performance, he almost had tears in his eyes and was, in his own words, devastated and lamented that you can't even trust little children these days.

He threw up his hands appealing to Allah for justice and restitution.

Unbelievable, I thought, I got conned twice within a few minutes. However, thinking back, this performance was worthy of an Oscar and well worth the five dollars.

We have been gouged and overcharged in a lot of places but this was an epic piece of well-orchestrated theatre. It was done with a lot of imagination you wouldn't be able to find in Toronto.

I enjoyed it.

✸ Chapter 14

My Travels With Tony

It's surprising what you can learn about your country of birth and its culture when you see it through someone else's eyes.

Tony was an amazing man with the unique gift of being both pretentious and humble at the same time while also being pompous, condescending, appreciative or wide-eyed astonished. He was extremely talented, highly educated and very successful as both an academic and a civil servant.

In 1987 the Canadian International Development Agency offered Tony an opportunity to work in Thailand. Over a nine month period he opened and developed a geological lab for the Thai government modelled after the one he ran in Toronto for the Province of Ontario.

I promised to show him Germany on his way back home.

We met up in Frankfurt and started our whirlwind tour of Germany and Austria.

Tony was well versed in the countries' history and culture and as a classical music lover. He adored opera and composers such as Wagner, Mozart, Bach and Beethoven.

I took him to all the places he was eager to see and the ones I felt were important for him to explore. We went on a day-cruise down the Rhine and he was humbled by the imposing castles and fortresses. He mentioned that the scenery brought the opera 'The Ring of the Nibelungen' by Richard Wagner to life in his imagination. To my astonishment he knew and hummed along to the Lorelei song played on the ship's public address system as we passed the imposing cliff known as the Lorelei, a famous part of Germanic folklore.

Heidelberg Castle, where Tony relived his favourite movie, 'The Student Prince' with Mario Lanza, was our next stop.

As we entered the cavernous wine cellar of the castle a choir started singing the famous song 'Drink, Drink, Drink'. He was overwhelmed and I saw him wiping a few tears off his face. The voices sounded magnificent as they echoed off the walls. We assumed they were a professional choir but it turned out to be a rather boisterous and slightly inebriated football team from Hamburg.

The next day we went on to the Bavarian Alps. Tony was fascinated by Neuschwanstein Castle, which was the inspiration for Disneyland's Sleeping Beauty Castle. He knew more than I did about Bavaria's Mad King Ludwig II, who had it built, and his admiration for Richard Wagner and his music. Neuschwanstein embodies both the contemporaneous architectural fashion known as castle romanticism (Burgenromantik), and Ludwig II's immoderate enthusiasm for the operas of Richard Wagner. In fact most of the rooms are themed after his operas. Everything about the castle, its sheer beauty, its location, its vistas are magical.

In Salzburg we spent half a day at Mozart's birth house. Tony was awed to be in the place where Wolfgang Amadeus Mozart grew up and paid homage to one of the greatest composers by reading every description and studying every exhibit.

It was a bit disappointing for me to see so few artifacts on display, old instruments he and his family used to play, a few manuscripts and furniture. I expected a Mozart soundtrack to be playing while roaming from room to room but the silence was deafening. It really was quite boring for me. I expected more. Tony felt differently. He absorbed every detail with great reverence.

We left Salzburg the next morning to spend a day in a real castle normally reserved for the rich and famous. Until then we had chosen small B&Bs and village inns for lodging but decided we would splurge for one night in a real medieval castle.

We chose Schloss Fuschl just outside of Salzburg.

It was built in 1461 as a hunting castle for the Archbishop of Salzburg on an exquisite spit of land stretching into Lake Fuschl. It was converted into a luxurious hotel in 1947. It quickly became a meeting point and playground for the rich and famous. Many heads of state, Nikita Khrushchev of the USSR, Anwar al-Sadat of Egypt, American President Gerald Ford as well as members of the royal families of Britain and Sweden, to name a few, have stayed at this idyllic resort.

Tony was in his element.

It is probably a good time to describe Tony's demeanour, especially when he was in his pretentious and sophisticated mode. Although the word metro-sexual didn't exist back in the 80s, Tony was the quintessential example of one, very expressive with gestures, well dressed, carried a man bag before it became hip and tended to prance slightly when walking.

To see him slowly meander along the lake or sit in one of the opulent couches in the foyer of the castle was a joy. His pose holding a cigarette while draping himself over the chaise lounge reminded me of Truman Capote.

He had a ball being surrounded by people possibly more pretentious than he was.

When it came to being flamboyant there was nobody better than Tony.

Dinner in the majestic dining hall was very memorable, unfortunately for all the wrong reasons. Unbeknownst to us we were introduced to Nouvelle Cuisine, where presentation reigns supreme but the food is very light and portions are tiny.

Famished from our long walk on the castle's well-manicured grounds and along the lake we were looking forward to a meal fit for a king.

When we saw the prices on the menu we swallowed hard. The cheapest item was a four-course set menu with three different options for each course.

The salad was a single leaf of lettuce with a radish, a slice of tomato and some other green leafy vegetable and a few drops of dressing.

The soup, a clear beef bouillon with a hint of truffle was served in a demitasse, that's a cup the size of an espresso. It came with a delicate thin cracker on the side.

Then came the main dish.

The waiters, wearing stylish 18th century uniforms, walked up next to us carrying a domed tray. The maitre d' stood at one side of our table and when the waiters were properly positioned he clapped his hands and in unison the waiters raised the bells from the tray to reveal the plate of food.

It was a painting!

Both of us had chosen the roast beef and it was presented on the plate as a painting of a face.

The hair was mashed potatoes so thin it must have been brushed on. The nose was a slice of carrot and the cheeks were two slices of roast beef you could actually see through. The eyes were slices of egg, the mouth was artistically shaped tomato slices and the left and right outlines of the face were two spears of asparagus.

It looked great but I didn't know if I was supposed to eat it or frame it and take it home to hang on my wall.

Starved after finishing the two forks full of food on my plate the waiter asked me what my choice for dessert was. I chose the Mozart Noodles assuming I would get a dish of sweet pasta to fill up on.

The two pieces of fusilli pasta with a sprinkling of cinnamon and a few drops and lines of chocolate sauce looked lost on my enormous dessert plate.

It was a lovely meal to look at but we were hungrier after the meal than before.

To drive to a nearby village to find a pub open and have a sausage or a schnitzel was our next move.

Luck was not on our side and we couldn't find a single village with a pub nor were there any stores open in Austria after 6:00 pm. Back to our room we went to raid the mini bar for all the potato chips, cookies and chocolate bars. We still went to bed hungry.

Looking out the window the next morning the blue sky and bright sunshine promised a beautiful day ahead but we were still hungry.

We decided to pack up and go to breakfast, which was included with our room, hoping to get a good cup of coffee and didn't count on more than a few crumbs of a low fat, healthy carrot muffin or maybe some muesli. Our expectations were not very high after our dinner experience. Instead we planned on having a hearty lunch in a good country inn on our drive back to Germany.

We didn't expect what we saw when we walked into the dining room.

The buffet had the most impressive selection of hams, cold cuts, cheeses, smoked fish and salads I've ever seen. There were cakes, tarts, an assortment of fruits and many varieties of breads and buns.

It was truly a buffet fit for a king.

Our stay was longer than anticipated and we could hardly move when we got up. We took it easy and stopped many times to take pictures of the beautiful countryside and arrived in Passau in the early afternoon, just in time to attend the afternoon organ concert in Passau's cathedral. The organ is the largest church organ in the world and was another highlight in what turned out to become Tony's musical odyssey of central Europe.

The concert, a selection of Bach cantatas, was short, just about thirty minutes, but the experience was unforgettable. Both of us were awestruck and emotionally uplifted by the incredible sound surrounding and engulfing us.

Looking for a room to spend the night we were lucky to find a reasonably priced, century-old inn right in the old part of town on the banks of the Danube river. It was Canadian Thanksgiving and Tony thought we should try to find a restaurant that served turkey. To our surprise the restaurant in our inn had breaded turkey breast with spaghetti on the menu.

We had a great meal, not exactly a traditional Thanksgiving meal, but sitting in this old inn overlooking the Danube at night put us in a reflective mood. We finished a couple of bottles of delicious Danube wines and reminisced about how thankful we were for our good fortune, both on this trip and in our lives.

Tony was eager to get up early the next morning because our next stop was Bayreuth and he wanted to have a truly Wagnerian experience.

The first thing Tony wanted to see was the Bayreuth Festspielhaus or Bayreuth Festival Theatre, an opera house built to the strict specifications of Richard Wagner and dedicated solely to the performance of his stage works.

Disappointment was written all over his face when we were told there would be no tours of the theatre that day because the orchestra had scheduled rehearsals.

I begged the person who looked like he was in charge to let us just have glimpse of the hall since rehearsals had not yet started. I must have been very persuasive because he called a janitor to open the door to allow us to have a look.

I am not sure that tours of the Bayreuth Festspielhaus are really of interest to anybody but those that love opera and in particular Wagner.

As far as I was concerned there was not much to see. The theatre was fairly ordinary, by no means opulent, without great decorations. Wagner designed it to have perfect acoustics. We stayed only a couple of minutes as the musicians started to arrive.

We then walked through the immaculate grounds of Wagner's estate to his grave for Tony to pay his respects. On our way to Wagner's home, an impressive villa he had named 'Wahnfried' (literally translated to 'freedom from madness') which is now a museum, we heard the orchestra practice.

We sat down to listen to them play. I wasn't allowed to talk during that time as Tony listened intensely with his eyes closed.

I admit to not having known much about the turbulent life of Richard Wagner, his music, his anti-Semitic views, his womanizing, his quite impoverished life during his exile from Germany and many other things that made his life fascinating. I was interested in the exhibits of the museum but had enough after two hours. Tony, just as in Mozart's house, was again studying every miniature model of every set design, every costume used in his operas and every manuscript and audio aid available.

I told him I had seen a pub just outside the grounds and would wait for him there.

I forgot if it was two or three hours later that he showed up still intoxicated with joy from having been privileged to have had this experience. I too was intoxicated by that time but more from the excellent beer I had while talking to locals.

After an early dinner we decided to drive straight through to Berlin where my good friends Horst and Annemarie were waiting for us. With no delays at the East German border the trip could be made in four hours. Luckily the ever unpredictable East German border guards were on our side that day and we arrived in Berlin at a reasonable time.

Horst and Annemarie welcomed us with open arms and made us feel very comfortable in their house. We would call it home for the next eight days.

Annemarie spoke almost no English. Horst had studied English quite a bit over the years. However it is fair to say it was a bit of a lost cause.

We had a few drinks and chatted a while, mostly with me translating. Tony probably understood more German from his knowledge of Dutch than Horst understood English.

I was tired after a long day and went to bed shortly after midnight.

The agenda of exciting things for us to see and do in Berlin was ambitious. Berlin is probably one of the most fascinating cities in the world,

But then I'm a bit biased.

The first day we took it easy.

Horst, who took early retirement at age 39 due to an injury he received while on duty as a firefighter, had bought a taxi in order not to die of boredom. He offered to give us a city tour of Berlin.

We took in all the touristy places and Tony was impressed with Horst's knowledge of the city, but also quite amused with his constant efforts to speak English and giving up in mid-sentence with the words, 'Konnie, you translate.'

When we came home that night Annemarie had a huge surprise for us.

She told one of her clients about our visit and mentioned that Tony was a huge opera fan. It just so happened that the world famous 'La Scala de Milano Opera Theatre' had a guest engagement at the German State Opera in Berlin the next day. Her client offered her a pair of tickets as a gift, no charge.

This was the event of the year and tickets were sold out the day they went on sale the previous year. The Scala de Milano is probably only rivalled by New York's Metropolitan Opera in fame and recognition around the world. We were stunned. We did not expect that this musical odyssey of ours would end with Verdi's masterpiece, Nabucco.

Both of us thanked Annemarie and our anonymous benefactor.

I was also quite excited since the chorus of the Hebrew slaves was my father's favourite piece of music. I explained to Tony that the chorus had a special meaning to Germans for the last 50 years.

'Die Gedanken sind frei', the German lyrics of the chorus for the Hebrew slaves, translated are;

The thoughts are free
I think as I please
And this gives me pleasure
My conscience decrees
This right I must treasure
My thoughts will not cater
To duke or dictator
No man can deny
Die Gedanken sind frei
Tyrants can take me
And throw me in prison
My thoughts will burst forth
Like blossoms in season
Foundations may crumble
And structures may tumble
But free men shall cry
Die Gedanken sind frei

During the Third Reich, as well as under the Communists, Germans would stand up during the song of the Hebrew slaves and sing along in defiance of the tyranny of the state to voice their opposition. Nabucco would be shunned by Hitler and after the war by the Communist Party because every time it was performed this form of protest and resistance occurred.

We got all dressed up in the only suits we brought and went to the opera the next day.

The outfits worn by Germans for the opera are still very much reminiscent of what you see in old movies. Tuxedos and black tails for men and lavish designer gowns for women. Champagne and caviar on crackers are sold in the lobby before the performance and during intermission, but pretzels, wieners and beer are also available to feed the less sophisticated and lower income patrons who show up in jeans and sweaters. Tony wanted to live it up and bought us champagne to lift us into the upper class of patrons. To him beer was not acceptable in these surroundings.

This was a truly unforgettable performance and we should have brought a box of Kleenex along. Tony had tears rolling down his face almost constantly and I was not far behind during the song of the Hebrew slaves.

This undoubtedly was Tony's highlight of our trip.

The next night we went to what is a must when in Berlin, a cabaret.

My choice was a classic transvestite show in a smoky, high-class, intimate club called Charlie Chez Nous. We had both seen the original movie La Cage aux Folles and I had been to Charlie Chez Nous before with Jackie and knew what to expect. Charlie Chez Nous is one of the most famous night clubs in Germany and a popular bar for celebrities, politicians and the in-crowd. We decided to take in the early show at 11:00 pm rather than the late show at 2:00 am. The nightlife in Berlin does not get started much before midnight. We had another grand night of breathtaking entertainment.

The Six Days of Berlin is a six-day cycling race held annually in Berlin. It was first held in 1909.

Tony could certainly not be described as a sports fan and was not too enthusiastic when I told him we'd be going to the bicycle races the following night. I think he only came along to keep me happy. That soon changed once we got into the velodrome. The crowd was again an assortment of people in jeans, casual clothes, tuxedos and evening gowns drinking beer or champagne while watching the race or partying in the infield of the velodrome. In the foyer and all around this big venue was a carnival atmosphere while on the track world-class cyclists competed in teams of two in this gruelling competition. One rider was always on the track while the other slept, drank, ate or did whatever he had to do when his partner was racing. At first Tony didn't know what was going on since there are many races within the race, sprints for points or bonuses, elimination races for cash prizes and much more. Tony, fascinated by the frantic activities, wanted to understand what was going on. While sipping on a glass of champagne he studied the rules, the race and the riders. It took him only a short time to find a Dutch team he could root for and before I knew it, he was completely engrossed in the race. He got into it with gusto.

I was completely flabbergasted when, after four hours at the races, I asked him to go home and he said,"Lets wait just until after the next point sprint. If the Dutch win it they'll be in first place overall and we can go home." It was probably the first and last time that he got emotionally involved in a professional sporting event. I can't remember if they won but assume they did because Tony went home very happy.

The next day was our visit to East Berlin. The contrast of the East to the West was shocking.

Propaganda banners were hung everywhere with praise for the first 'German Workers and Farmers State' and the Communist party. Huge posters were proclaiming friendship and solidarity with the USSR. There was little traffic on the road, and bomb damage from the war was still visible in many houses.

The restaurants were offering a limited selection of substandard quality food on their menus and many stores were operating with literally nothing to sell. People did not look happy in their mostly drab and unfashionable clothing. As we walked around Alexander Platz, a famous square in Berlin, he spotted a book store with some interesting and good looking coffee-table books in their window display. We went in and asked how much they cost. The clerk told us that they were not for sale. Only communist propaganda, party handbooks and a few novels with patriotic themes were available for purchase.

In those days it was mandatory to exchange a certain amount of western currency, about $20.00, into East German marks in order to enter the DDR. You had to spend it before you left because exporting East German currency into the West was illegal. East Germans would not change your currency back to West marks or dollars either. You were forced to spend it upon leaving the DDR or donate it to the Vietnam Peace Fund supporting the Vietcong.

On our way to the train station we decided to eat a knackwurst from one of the street vendors. When he heard me ordering in perfect German but conversing with Tony in English he got curious asking us where we were from. After we told him we were Canadians he began ranting quite sarcastically and facetiously about the East German Government and Communism.

It turned out he was an academic with a PhD who refused to join the Communist Party and support or praise their programs. He lost his job and was forced to sell knackwurst and wieners on a street corner to support his family. In a loud voice he yelled and ranted for everybody to hear: "You tell your friends in the West what a great country this is. The state has allowed me to sell substandard sausages infused with water to make them look juicy and fat. Be careful when you bite into them, water might squirt all over your clothes. Yes, things might look good in our republic but don't prick the surface."

After paying him for the two sausages we gave him all our East German money, keeping just enough to buy our train ticket back to the West. We certainly didn't want to hang around to see him being arrested. Wishing him well we could see the desperation and disgust in his eyes. He thanked us and tried to smile as we left. It was a sad way to leave this once glorious part of the city.

The last two days were spent exploring more of this vibrant city and having a ball. When it was time to say good-bye to Berlin, my friends and relatives, all of us decided to have a final Aufwiedersehen Party in Berlin's Renaissance fortress, the Spandau Citadel. As you enter the impressive fortress, it's easy to imagine the sounds of the past – the neighing of horses and shouts of medieval knights.

In these walls, the Renaissance era truly comes alive. They offered a 14th century meal in the fortress' dungeon with authentic utensils, drinking chalices and waiters and waitresses dressed in period clothing. We ate with our fingers and drank mead, a fermented honey based drink, out of a bucket served by a wench who would ladle it right into our mouths. Wine was served in real bullhorns, plates were made of wood. Jesters, musicians and jugglers entertained us the whole night.

It was an unforgettable evening.

Let me correct that. Tony might have forgotten whole parts of it. He could not get enough of the mead and we had a tough time getting him home. I never saw him drunk before or since, but that night he let loose and really enjoyed himself.

Getting up early the next morning after only three hours sleep to fly back to Toronto was difficult. Tony could not wake up to say good-bye due to what appeared to be a slight case of alcohol poisoning. I didn't feel that great myself but managed to tame the guy who was swinging that sledgehammer in my head after having a cold shower and a few cups of coffee.

Annemarie told me when I called her the next day that Tony woke up at about 1:00 pm and she took him for a walk through Berlin's famous Tiergarten Park and basically told him to breath and walk very slowly so not to upset his slowly recovering system from the wild night we had before. She and Horst made sure he got to the airport for his late flight to London where he stayed for a few days before flying home from his long journey around the world.

I had one of the best times of my life with Tony and asked him on his deathbed what his highlight was of our trip. He smiled and said just one word, "Nabucco."

Anthony H. Marinus "Tony" Vander Voet
1945 - 2018

Chapter 15

My Day In A Mexican Jail
OR
Guilty Of Driving While Canadian

Pointy, our friend from Canada, was in town with his new girlfriend Linda and we went out on a drive to show them our Mexican winter paradise in the Yucatan.

Pointy had rented a condo near us and this was a combination orientation and sightseeing trip with a lunch planned at the beautiful beach in Progresso. We picked them up at about 10:00 am and drove off.

Most roads in and out of Progresso are one-way streets. Driving down a main road I slowly moved over to the left-hand side of the road to make a left turn. I had driven about 50 meters on the left-hand side of the two-lane street and as I started to turn a red Toyota hit me, denting my door slightly and taking my rear-view mirror off.

I admit I didn't see the Toyota coming and did not look into my mirror because I was already on the left-hand side of the paved road with only a sand strip to my left.

The driver, an older lady, had driven off the road onto the sandy strip to pass me and hit me just as I started turning. Her car hardly had any damage, just a scratch on her bumper. She became very agitated and frustrated by my limited Spanish and her non-existent English. She immediately got on her cell phone and called the police.

Fine, I thought, I didn't do anything wrong, let the police come.

Within minutes three police cars arrived and when it became clear we had a communication problem a fourth car with a bilingual officer arrived.

He took my version of events and told me to give him the keys to my car.

He explained to me that it is the law in Mexico that neither one of the parties will be allowed to leave until the question of guilt and innocence had been decided and I was not even allowed to drive my car to the police station. All of us crammed into the rental car and the officer drove us to the main station in a neighbouring town.

My wife Jackie, Pointy and his girlfriend, were told to sit in the lobby and wait.

By now it was about 11:30 am.

The next scene was like something out of those Mexican gangster movies.

I was led into an office where, I guess a higher ranking officer, was sitting with his feet on his desk, watching a movie on a small 17" television set perched on a filing cabinet next to him. He just waved at me to sit down and kept on watching the movie laughing uncontrollably every few seconds.

After a few minutes and a few laughs he turned to me and started asking me for my name and where I lived. When I told him I lived in the small village of Chicxulub his eyes lit up. He told me that his brother was a fisherman in Chicxulub and asked if I would be interested in buying shrimp from him.

Not really waiting for my answer he said: " How many kilos would you like to buy?"

"Gee, I would have to ask my wife, but we are interested because we eat a lot of shrimp."

My reply brought a smile to his face and he gave me his brother's address and mentioned that he would check to see if I had gone to see him.

Good, a little bit of extortion here, I thought.

The interrogation continued and he asked me why I didn't signal. I told him I did and that I was already driving on the left side of the road and the lady had to drive on the unpaved, sandy shoulder to pass me.

My mention that I had three witnesses in the lobby who could verify my testimony just got a mild shoulder shrug and no indication that he would follow-up with them.

My interrogation was now finished and he called in a young policeman to take me away. As I was leaving he still reminded me to buy shrimp from his brother and he would let him know that I was coming around.

The young officer led me around a corner and there, along a corridor, were four jail cells.

The cell at the end was occupied by a not so friendly and rough-looking Mexican. I was put into the first cell.

It is an understatement to say that I was not happy and started to worry a bit. I was told to sit down and then the policeman left without closing the cell door behind him.

It was almost 1:00 pm by now and I was getting hungry. There was nobody around, the corridor was empty. I wondered if I was allowed to go to the corner to call somebody since my door was open. My imagination ran wild. What if somebody thought I was trying to escape, they might shoot first and ask questions later.

My subdued calls for somebody were not answered so I slowly crept to the end of the corridor to get somebody's attention.

The young policeman was talking to another officer at the end of the hall.

After a couple of hellos he noticed me and sent the other officer to talk to me.

He said I was free to leave the cell and was put there only because they didn't have a waiting room and, as long as I didn't leave the station, I was free to see my friends in the lobby.

There was no cafeteria and Jackie got some change to get me a Coke and a bag of chips out of a vending machine.

When we inquired how long this would take we were told they were waiting for my insurance agent to arrive from Merida to settle the question of damages. After that I would see a magistrate who would rule on whose fault the accident was. We would be allowed to leave after his verdict.

Pointy asked if he would be allowed to leave but I asked him to stay because I might need him as a witness.

The insurance man arrived at 4:30 pm. He spoke perfect English.

The good news he gave me was that the insurance I had covered everything and the bad news was that the police had decided it was my fault.

I started arguing with him but he stopped me right away.

"Look", he said," I am just here to assess damages and let you know that we will pay. You can tell your story to the magistrate."

When I asked him why they wouldn't even question my witnesses and why they had decided the accident was my fault he said that her story was possibly more believable.

I replied that he meant that I was guilty because I was not Mexican.

He just shrugged his shoulders.

It was almost 6:00 pm when I was led into a room where another important looking Mexican man in an important looking uniform sat behind an impressive looking desk.

He looked at me and said in broken but understandable English: "I find you guilty of causing accident. Fine is 900 Pesos."

That was it? He was judge, jury and prosecutor?

I didn't know how to address him. Recalling all my Perry Mason knowledge I said, "Your Honour, I don't know what I am being accused of, I didn't do anything wrong."

"Okay, okay, okay," he replied, "700 Pesos."

Before I could ask him if that was his final offer he got up and left.

I paid my fine, signed a few papers and was allowed to leave.

Free, free, free at last!

Chapter 15

The Final Journey

I guess everybody has thought and talked about how they would want to leave this world and how their final journey, to wherever they are going, should start. Just slipping away in your sleep or suddenly dropping dead is everybody's choice. A prolonged illness and a painful end is dreaded by everybody.

Iris Robertson showed me and others that we have a choice when saying good-bye and make leaving this world easy on yourself and your loved ones.

Iris knew how to live and Iris knew how to die.

We got to know Iris in Mexico. She stayed at Coral Beach, the same apartment complex we stay in during the winter months.

There are people who always become the focal point in any company and Iris was such a person.

She didn't walk, but practically floated into a room to immediately become the centre of attention. Everybody felt drawn to her warm personality and the twinkle in her eyes told of her great sense of humour. That humour could hold a healthy dose of sarcasm, but she was always generous, caring and the life of any party. She dressed in the most fashionable and flamboyant flowing gowns.

No jeans or T-shirts for this lady.

Iris visited Chicxulub for the last time in 2016 and announced that this would probably be her last time since her health was failing.

It was a Friday night, the 8th of September 2017 when I received a call from Jacqueline Szorady, another good friend from our little Snowbird community in Mexico, letting me know that Iris was giving a farewell party that Sunday afternoon and asked for Jackie and me to attend.

Her congenital heart disease and COPD had progressed to a point where life was no longer enjoyable and she had decided to leave this world on her own terms with the help of a group of doctors who would assist her dying in a dignified and painless way.

Jackie and I agreed to go but were not looking forward to what we thought would be a morbid, depressing affair.

It turned out to be anything but morbid or depressing. Iris's farewell party was one of the most uplifting experiences I've ever been privileged to be part of.

When her family wheeled her into the party room of her condo building Iris, still dressed to kill, looked frail but there was still that sparkle in her eyes and she was clearly enjoying the attention and talked to everybody, remembering everybody's name.

Anybody who felt awkward and intimidated soon lost his or her inhibitions. Iris made all of us feel comfortable and relaxed with her humorous and casual approach to why we had gathered there that afternoon.

This was not supposed to be a somber, tearful gathering of doom but a celebration of life.

There was no sadness but laughter, stories and songs. Iris talked about her imminent departure like she was planning her next trip to Mexico.

She talked about her upcoming last minutes, that she disliked one of the two doctors who was going to administer the needle and demanded he be ushered away from her so he is not the last person she sees. She also refused to have the intravenous port inserted the night before and stubbornly insisted that she wouldn't spend her last night with an intravenous in her arm and they should bloody well arrange for the nurse to come early in the morning and prep her then.

She talked about selling her apartment a couple of days earlier and the complications that could arise from her dying in her apartment because of a local regulation that obliges you to reveal if there has ever been a dead body found in the apartment. An affirmative answer might jeopardize the closing which was scheduled a few days after her death. Her daughter, who lived in the same building, agreed to have the procedure performed in her apartment.

Iris had planned to be surrounded by her family and one of her sons and one grandson would play 'Red River Valley', her favourite song, while the needle is administered and it would be the last thing she heard when she closed her eyes.

There will be no prayers or tears. Iris will leave this world on her own terms, with dignity and knowing she lived life to the fullest, refusing to end it in pain and misery.

What a lady.

Friends and relatives said a few words and I passed along greetings from out-of-town members of our snowbird community in Mexico as we said our good-byes.

Jackie crouched down to give her a farewell kiss and said, "Good-bye Iris, we'll meet again on the other side." Iris sat straight up and, with a strong voice, said, "I don't believe in all that stuff about the other side, let's just say good-bye."

I leaned over to give her a hug and jokingly said, "Well Iris, how about coming back as a ghost and haunting everybody in Coral Beach?"

I saw that twinkle in her eyes as she smiled at me and said, "Now there's an Idea!"

I had dreaded that afternoon but I am glad Jackie and I went.

It was a great lesson of how to die with dignity and attending a living wake sure beats standing around a coffin and staring at a cold and lifeless body.

Not everybody would opt to end his or her own life when there is no more hope and only pain and suffering ahead but I am glad Canada made assisted dying a legal option.

I don't know if I will have the strength to go through with it but the following account of her last day as told by her daughter makes me proud to have known her and might give me the courage to make my own departure an uplifting and maybe even a joyous occasion.

I'd be much happier knowing that people will remember me as somebody who tried to have fun, be content and happy about his life until he took his last breath, just like Iris.

Here is her daughter Sherry's account of Iris's life and her last day on this earth:

> My mother was very proud of her decision and wanted the world to know about "dying with dignity". I know she would love me to share the details of her final day.
>
> My mom had been up most of the night prior, and in the morning had decided that her final meal would be bacon and eggs, since her salt-free diet had prevented her from consuming bacon for months. With great care, my brother Joe made her bacon and then perfectly done sunny side up eggs. When he walked over to serve it, he tripped on her oxygen hosing, and dropped the glass plate which smashed into pieces with egg and bacon everywhere. She thought it was funny and of course made some sarcastic remark.
>
> I bathed my mother, helped with her hair and make-up and dressed her. She wore a pure white gauzy top and pants that she had picked out and I had washed and ironed. Of course it was a stylish outfit.
>
> As she was so exhausted and was having trouble focusing, I had concerns about her answering critical last questions posed by the doctors performing the procedure. She had not been referring to it as a procedure; she said she was "offing herself". I role played with her beforehand, pretending to be the doctor, I asked "How are you Mrs Robertson?" and she said "How the 'F' do you think I am?!" If she was incoherent during the questions, the doctors would call the whole thing off.
>
> When my three brothers and their wives assembled at around 11am, we gave her a few sips of wine (which she hadn't had in months) and wheeled her down to my unit in the same building to get her ready. I had lots of flowers, including a big bouquet of irises scattered around my condo and many candles burning.

We got her settled on my white sofa with lots of white pillows, and a fluffy white blanket. With her pretty white outfit on, and against all the white, she looked so fresh, serene and almost angelic....she would probably say that was a stretch but that is how she looked to me. I was incredulous that my mother started to nod off with all of the commotion around her.

The nurse arrived and as we had all feared, had a problem finding a vein. The doctors had warned us that if this happened the procedure would be cancelled. We had two sister-in-laws who are nurses, and my brother who is a doctor trying to assist for about 15 minutes. The nurse was beet red in the face and sweating from all of the pressure, and literally, like in a movie, got the IV going a couple of minutes before the doctors arrived.

During this time two brothers were playing guitar and singing 'Red River Valley'. Even though it hurt her trying to locate a vein, my mom only winced a couple of times, but other than that, was completely calm and happy. Unbelievably calm in fact. We all took turns kissing her, holding her hand and brushing her hair back, and saying our final goodbyes. Through all the chaos of so many people in such a small space, she seemed so content that it would be over and was resolute in her decision, and pleased that the time had come. I asked her if she was nervous, anxious or scared, and she said not in the least.

Finally the doctors arrived. I was holding my breath as the doctor she didn't like crouched down beside her, readying to ask his required questions. She looked right at him before he started and said, "Oh, look it's Dr. Crabby!". We all laughed and I think given his young age and perhaps lack of experience, it unnerved him. Then he asked how she was and she said, "Great, I just had some wine". Oh, oh!

He asked her if she was drunk and she said she only had a couple of sips. He then asked questions such as, "Do you know what is going to happen?". She said "I don't want to know what is going to happen, continue with the other questions." He confirmed that she was not coerced, and that this was her decision, that it would be final, that the coroner would be called, etc.

The doctors prepared their tray with a cocktail of drugs including two large syringes of Propofol. When he said he was about to start she asked that the four of us (her children) stand in front of her so she could look at us as she died. She told us she loved us and to look after each other. She only wanted us to be sad for five minutes and then to be happy and celebrate. We told her that we loved her and said goodbye for the last time. We stood shoulder to shoulder, and through our tears everyone in the room sang 'Hallelujah' a cappella.

That was the only time her eyes were slightly moist, but she was still unbelievably brave and calm. As the second syringe was injected she started slipping away as we continued to sing 'Hallelujah'. One of my brothers who is hearing impaired, and can lip read said that she mouthed, "Very peaceful," as she was dying.

Although it may sound odd to some, it was a beautiful, tranquil death. It was just what she had hoped for. There was no choking, no shuddering or gasping. She closed her eyes and continued to rest on her pillow. It was like she had just fallen asleep. My brother Danny crossed her hands and pulled the blanket up, and gently placed her in a lying position on the couch.

The doctors then notified the coroner and we waited for the final sign-off from him, which seemed to take about half-an-hour, and then the doctors left. My brother called the Aftercare Company to retrieve her and they advised that it may be up to three hours.

Given our last name is Robertson, we had always assumed that we were Scottish until my brother Joe recently had his ancestry DNA done and discovered we are 48% Irish. So in true Irish tradition, albeit unplanned, this then turned into a true Irish wake. We uncorked the wine, poured Fireball, drank whiskey and tequila. We cheered to my mom, told stories about her, both good and bad. Talked about some of the outrageous and hysterical things she had said and done. We cried and we laughed while she laid peacefully beside us. She would have absolutely loved it, all of it!

When she was picked up, around 3:30 pm my brother Danny

escorted her to the vehicle. We then went back up to her condo and carried on drinking, celebrating and crying.

My mom wanted to die with dignity, and that she did. The whole event was so seamless, and events just fell into place and it seemed that on that day, September 11th, the universe unfolded as it should.

I am left with the realization that there is never any need to suffer at the end of your life, which in turn makes the loved ones around you suffer as well. The entire procedure seemed like a dream because it was so perfect. Watching my mom die so peacefully has given me a feeling of unexpected calmness. Although I am very sad, I am happy she chose this method of death, or as she called it "offing herself". I am grateful that she will never gasp for breath again.

My mother was a character, a handful at times, but entertained us, was hysterically funny, driven, ambitious, fearless, had a great sense of adventure, but mostly a great zest for life. I don't know of anyone at 87 who has packed that much living in. She raised five kids, was a great accomplished cook, (her apple pies were to die for), was fixing up and flipping homes by herself, before it was even a thing.

Travelled the world many times over, relishing the culture and history of each and every country she visited and travelling with both my brother Ben and myself on many occasions.

She ran a Bed and Breakfast by herself in her 70s. Was always attending film festivals, operas and socializing. Everyone who met her, loved her and adored her, even when her verbal filter didn't always engage. I asked her if there was anything left on her bucket list, and she said that she would have liked to see Poland, but other than that, she felt accomplished and there was nothing at all she yearned to do or see. A rich tapestry of life she had woven.

Good bye Iris.
I am a better person for having known you!